LIFE IS REAL ONLY THEN, WHEN 'I AM'

ALL AND EVERYTHING

G. I. Gurdjieff's

SANAGE
PUBLISHING HOUSE

Hardback: 978-939492458-1

Any references to historical events, real people, or real places are used fictitiously. Names, characters, and places are products of the author's imagination.

Printed by:

Sanage Publishing House LLP
Mumbai, India

sanagepublishing@gmail.com

George Ivanovich Gurdjieff (1866–1877–29 October 1949) was a Russian philosopher, mystic, spiritual teacher, and composer of Armenian and Greek descent, born in Alexandropol, Russian Empire (now Gyumri, Armenia). For some twenty years, he travelled in the remotest regions of Central Asia and the Middle East - this time was crucial in the moulding of his thought. With his party of followers, he was responsible for the opening of the Institute for the Harmonious Development of Man.

ALL AND EVERYTHING

Ten Books in Three Series

FIRST SERIES: Three books under the title of "Beelzebub's Tales to His Grandson" or "An Objectively Impartial Criticism of the Life of Man,"

SECOND SERIES: Three books under the common title of "Meetings with Remarkable Men."

THIRD SERIES: Four books under the common title of "Life Is Real Only Then, When I Am."

All written according to entirely new principles of logical reasoning and strictly directed towards the solution of the following three cardinal problems:

FIRST SERIES: To destroy, mercilessly, without any compromises whatsoever, in the mentation and feelings of the reader, the beliefs and views, by centuries rooted in him, about everything existing in the world.

SECOND SERIES: To acquaint the reader with the material required for a new creation and to prove the soundness and good quality of it.

THIRD SERIES: To assist the arising, in the mentation and in the feelings of the reader, of a veritable, nonfantastic representation not of that illusory world which he now perceives, but of the world existing in reality.

"No one interested in my writings should ever attempt to read them in any other than the indicated order; in other words, he should never read anything written by me before he is already well acquainted with the earlier works."

G. I. GURDJIEFF

"... as regards the real, indubitably comprehensible, genuine objective truths which will be brought to light by me in the third series, I intend to make them accessible exclusively only to those from among the hearers of the second series of my writings who will be selected by specially prepared people according to my considered instructions."

G. I. GURDJIEFF, Beelzebub's Tales to His Grandson (Third Book, p. 428)

CONTENTS

PROLOGUE

I am.. .? But what has become of that full sensing of the whole of myself, formerly always in me in just such cases of self-questioning during the process of self-remembering. . ..

Is it possible that this inner ability was achieved by me thanks to all kinds of self-denial and frequent self-goading only in order that now, when its influence for my Being is more necessary even than air, it should vanish without trace? No! This cannot be! . . . Something here is not right!

If this is true, then everything in the sphere of reason is illogical.

But in me is not yet atrophied the possibility of actualizing conscious labor and intentional suffering! . . .

According to all past events I must still be. I wish! .. . and will be!!

Moreover, my Being is necessary not only for my personal egoism but also for the common welfare of all humanity.

My Being is indeed necessary to all people; even more necessary to them than their felicity and their happiness of today. I wish still to be ... I still am!

By the incomprehensible laws of the association of human thoughts, now, before beginning to write this book which will be my third that is, my instructive series of writings, and in general my last book, through which I wish to share with the other creatures of our Common Father similar to myself almost all the previously unknown mysteries of the inner world of man which I have accidentally learned, there has reoccurred to me the above-quoted self-reasoning which proceeded in me during an almost delirious state exactly seven years ago today, and even, it seems to me, at this very hour.

This fantastic soliloquy proceeded in me the 6th of November 1927, early in the morning in one of the Montmartre night cafes in Paris when, tired already to exhaustion from my "black" thoughts, I had decided to go home and there once more to try whether I might perhaps succeed in sleeping at least a little.

Although my health was, then too, in general bad yet on this morning I felt particularly miserable.

My miserable state on that morning was also further aggravated by the fact that during the last two or three weeks I had slept not more than one or two hours in twenty-four, and this last night I had not been able to sleep at all.

The fundamental cause of such sleeplessness and general disorder, in those days already excessive, of nearly all the important functions of my organism, was the uninterrupted flowing in my consciousness of "heavy" thoughts about the apparently insoluble situation which had then unexpectedly arisen for me.

In order to be able to explain, at least approximately, what this insoluble situation for me was, I must first say the following:

For more than three years up till then I had been writing, almost day and night, with constant self-driving, the books I had resolved to publish.

I say with constant self-driving because, due to the consequences of an automobile accident which happened to me just before beginning to write these books, I had been very ill and weak, and therefore, of course, had not had the possibility tor any active action.

Yet I had not spared myself, and had worked very hard in such a state, chiefly thanks to the factors that formed in my consciousness, from the very beginning, the following *idee fixe* notion:

Since I had not, when in full strength and health, succeeded in introducing in practice into the life of people the beneficial truths elucidated for them by me, then I must at least, at any cost, succeed in doing this in theory, before my death.

While writing out in outline during the first year the different fragments intended for publication, I had decided to write three series of books.

I had decided with the contents of the first series of books to achieve the destruction, in the consciousness and feelings of people, of deep rooted convictions which in my opinion are false and quite contradictory to reality.

With the contents of the second series of books to prove that there exist other ways of perceiving reality, and to indicate their direction.

With the contents of the third series of books to share the possibilities which I had discovered of touching reality and, if so desired, even merging with it.

With such intentions I began from the second year to write out this material in definite books, in a form now for general understanding.

And just before the events I am now describing, I had finished writing all the books of the first series and was already working on the books of the second series.

As I had the intention of publishing the first series of my writings the following year, I therefore decided, parallel with working on the books of the second series, to hold frequent public readings of the first series.

I decided to do this in order, before finally sending them to press, to review them once more but this time in accordance with the impressions with which different fragments were received by people of different typicality's and different degrees of mental development.

And in view of this aim, I began from then on to invite to my city apartment different persons of my acquaintance of corresponding individuality to hear the chapter proposed for correction, which was read aloud by somebody in their presence.

At that time, I had my principal place of residence for my whole family as well as for myself at Fontainebleau, but because of my frequent visits to Paris I was obliged also to have an apartment there.

During these common readings, in the presence of listeners of many different typicalities, while simultaneously observing the audience and listening to my writing, now ready for publication, I for the first time very definitely established and clearly, without any doubt, understood the following:

The form of the exposition of my thoughts in these writings could be understood exclusively by those readers who, in one way or another, were already acquainted with the peculiar form of my mentation.

But every other reader for whom, strictly speaking, I had goaded myself almost day and night during this time, would understand nearly nothing.

During this common reading, by the way, I enlightened myself for the first time with regard to the particular form in which it would be necessary to write in order that it might be accessible to the understanding of everyone.

So, when I had clarified all this to myself, there just then appeared before me, in all its splendor and full majesty, the question of my health.

Above everything else, there then flowed in my consciousness the following thoughts:

If all this, which was written during three or four years of almost unceasing day and night work, were to be rewritten from the beginning in another form more accessible to the understanding of every reader, at least the same length of time would be required. . ... But time is needed for the exposition of the second and third series; and time will be also necessary for introducing into practical life the essence of these writings of mine. . ... But where can so much time be obtained? . . .

If my time depended solely upon me I could, of course, rewrite all this anew. Moreover, from the very beginning of this new writing, I would acquire the certainty of a peaceful end, for now, knowing how to write, I could fully expect that at least after my death the principal aims of my life would certainly be realized.

But, due to all kinds of accumulated consequences of my past life, it so happens that just now my time depends not upon me but exclusively upon the "self-willed" Archangel Gabriel. And indeed, there remains to me but one or two or perhaps, at the most, three years more of life.

Concerning this, that is, that I have soon to die, any one of hundreds of physician-specialists knowing me can now confirm.

Besides this, I myself in my past life had not in vain been known as a good, above the average, diagnostician.

Not for nothing had I during my life held many conversations with thousands of candidates for a speedy departure from this world.

It would, strictly speaking, even be unnatural if it were not so . . . For the processes of the involution of my health during my past life had proceeded many times more rapidly and intensively than the processes of its evolution.

In fact, all the functions of my organism which previously had been, as my friends said, "steel-cast," had gradually degenerated, so that at the present moment due to constant overworking not one of them was, even relatively, functioning properly.

This is not at all to be wondered at. ... Even without considering the many other events unusual in human experience which had taken place in the accidentally peculiar pattern of my past life, it would be enough to recall that strange and inexplicable destiny pursuing me, which consisted in my having been wounded three times in quite different circumstances, each time almost mortally and each time by a stray bullet.

If the full significance of only these three incidents were comprehended, which inevitably implanted ineffaceable results in my body, one could understand that they in themselves were sufficient to have caused my final end long ago.

The first of these three incomprehensible fateful events happened in 1896, on the island of Crete, one year before the Greco-Turkish War.

From there, while still unconscious, I was brought, I don't know why, by some unknown Greeks to Jerusalem.

Soon, with consciousness returned, although with my health not yet quite restored, I in the company of other just such as myself "seekers of pearls in manure" set out from Jerusalem for Russia not by water, as normal people ordinarily do, but by land, on foot.

From such wandering, continuing about four months nearly always through places almost impassable, with my health still in precarious condition, there must, of course, have been implanted in my organism for the rest of my life some "chronically manifesting" factors of evil influence upon my health.

In addition to everything else, during this foolish trip, there visited me and found delight in my body, for quite a long stay, some specific "delicacies" of local character, among which, by the way, were the honored and famous "Kurdistan tzinga" (scurvy), the not less famous "Armenian dysentery" and, of course, that common and omnipresent favorite of many names: *la grippe,* or influenza.

After this, willy-nilly, I had to live some months, without absenting myself, at home in Transcaucasia, and then again began, animated of course as always by the *idee fixe* of my inner world, various trips through all kinds of bush and jungle.

And this time in my unfortunate physical body I again played host, during their long visits, to many other specific delicacies of local character.

Among such new guests were the honored "Ashkhabadian bedinka," "Bokharian malaria," "Tibetan hydropsy," "Beluchistan dysentery" and many others who also left their calling cards permanently whenever they called.

In the following years my organism, although it had already acquired immunity from all such local delicacies, nevertheless could not, of course, due to its increasing tenseness, eradicate the consequences of these old delicacies.

Under such conditions of tension years passed; then, for this unfortunate physical body of mine, came another year of destiny, 1902, when I was punctured by a second stray bullet.

This occurred in the majestic mountains of Tibet one year before the Anglo-Tibetan War.

On this second occasion, my unfortunate physical body was able to elude destiny because near me there were five good physicians three of European education and two specialists of Tibetan medicine, all five very sincerely devoted to me.

After three or four months of unconscious life, for me there flowed still another year of constant physical tenseness and unusual psychic contrivance and then came my third fateful year.

This was at the end of 1904 in the Transcaucasian region in the neighborhood of the Chiatura Tunnel.

Speaking about this third stray bullet, I cannot here deny myself the opportunity, for the pleasure of some and for the displeasure of others of my acquaintances of the present time, of now saying openly about this third bullet that it was plunked into me, of course unconsciously, by some "charmer" from among those two groups of people, who, fallen on one side under the influence of the revolutionary psychosis and on the other under the sway of imperious superiors, accidental upstarts, together laid then, also of course unconsciously, the basic foundation stones of the groundwork of the, at least today, indeed "great Russia."

There then proceeded firing between the so-called Russian army, chiefly Cossacks, and the so-called Gourians.

In view of the fact that certain events in my life, beginning with this third nearly fatal wound and up to the present time, have among themselves, as I have recently noticed, a very strange, and at the same time very definite, connection in terms of one physical law, I will therefore describe some of these events with as much detail as possible.

It is necessary before going further to mention here also that on the evening of November 6, 1927, when, after a good sleep, I began to think of the situation that had arisen for me, then into my consciousness flashed one idea, among others, which then appeared to me entirely absurd; but now, after having constated unexpectedly and having elucidated during the last seven years various facts previously unknown to me, I have become convinced without any doubt that it must be true.

And so, at the time of this third bullet, near me there was only one man, and at that a very weak one. As I learned later, he, surmising that the situation and surrounding circumstances were such that very undesirable consequences might arise for me, quickly somewhere found a donkey and, placing me, completely unconscious, on it, in haste drove it far into the mountains.

There he put me in some cave, and himself went to look for help.

He found some kind of a "barber-physician" and necessary bandages and returned with them late in the evening.

They did not find anyone in the cave and were astounded, because neither could I have left by myself nor could anyone else have come there, and as far as wild animals were concerned, they knew well that in this region, aside from deer and goat and sheep, there were no animals.

They noticed traces of blood, but it was impossible to follow them because the night had already fallen.

Only the next morning, when it began to dawn, after spending the whole night in anxiety and fruitless search in the forest did they find me between some rocks, still alive and apparently sound asleep.

The barber immediately found some roots, and with these he made a temporary tourniquet, and after giving instructions to my weak friend what to do, he at once set out somewhere.

Late in the evening he returned accompanied by two of his friends, called "Khevsurs," with a two-wheeled cart to which were harnessed two mules.

That evening they drove me still higher into the mountains and again placed me in a cave, but this time a large one, adjacent to another immense cave in which, as later appeared, sat and reclined, perhaps contemplating human life of past and future ages, several score Khevsurian dead, "mummified" by the rarefied air of that high place.

In this cave where they placed me, for two weeks, in the presence of the aforementioned weak man, the barber and one young Khevsur, there proceeded in me the struggle between life and death.

After that my health began to improve at such a pace that in one week more my consciousness had entirely returned, and I could already move about with the help of someone and a stick, and a couple of times even visit the "secret meeting" of my "immortal neighbors."

At this time, it was ascertained that below, in the process of civil war, the upper hand, as it is said, had been taken by the Russian army and that already everywhere the Cossacks were poking about and arresting every "suspicious" inhabitant who was not a native.

As I was not a native and also knew the process of the mentation of people fallen under a "revolutionary psychosis," I decided to flee from these parts as soon as possible.

Taking into consideration the surrounding conditions of the Transcaucasian region as a whole, and my personal prospects for the future, I decided to go into the Transcaspian region.

Subjected to incredible physical sufferings, I set out in the company of the above-mentioned weak man.

I experienced unbelievable sufferings chiefly because I had everywhere on the way to preserve an unsuspicious exterior.

An exterior not arousing suspicion was necessary so as not to become a victim either of this "political psychosis" or of the so-called "national psychosis."

The fact of the matter is that, in places where the railroad passed, there had only recently been completed a so-called "realization of a higher gradation" of the "national psychosis," in this instance between the Armenians and Tartars, and some peculiarities of this human scourge still continued to flow by momentum.

My misfortune in this case consisted in the fact that, having a "universal appearance," I represented to the Armenians a pure-blooded Tartar and to the Tartars a pure-blooded Armenian.

To make a long story short, I, by hook or by crook, in the company of this weak friend of mine, and with the help of a "mouth harmonica," arrived in the Transcaspian region.

This mouth harmonica, which I discovered in the pocket of my coat, rendered us a great service.

On this original instrument I then played, I confess, not badly although I played only two tunes: "The Peaks of Manchuria" and "Valse Ozhidanie."

Arriving in the Transcaspian region we decided for the time being to establish ourselves in the city of Ashkhabad.

We rented two good rooms in a private house with a charming garden, and I could finally rest.

Yet, on the first morning when my only near person there went to a pharmacy to get for me the necessary medicaments, he did not return for a long time.

Hours passed, but still he did not come ... he did not come.

I began to be anxious, chiefly because I knew that he was here for the first time and did not yet know anybody.

Night is falling and I have no more patience. ... I am going to look for him.

But where? First of all, I go to the pharmacy. There they know nothing. . . .

Suddenly, listening to my questions, the druggist's boy says that he saw this same young man, who was there in the morning, arrested by the police in the street not far from there, and taken away somewhere.

What is to be done? Where to go? I know no one here, and besides I am hardly able to move because during the last few days I have become completely exhausted.

When I leave the pharmacy, it is almost completely dark in the street. By chance an unoccupied carriage passes. I ask to be taken to the center of the city, somewhere near the bazaar where after the stores close there is still life.

I decide to go to such a place in the hope of meeting, perhaps in one of the cafes or *chaikhanas*, someone of my acquaintance.

I am barely moving through narrow streets, and come across only small *ashkhanas*, where only the Tekinians sit.

I am weakening more and more, and in my thoughts already flashes a suspicion that I may lose consciousness.

I sit down on the terrace in front of the first *chaikhana* I pass and ask for some green tea.

While drinking tea, I come to thank God! and look around on the space dimly lit by the street lantern.

I see a tall man with a long beard, in European clothing, pass by the *chaikhana*.

His face seems familiar. I stare at him while he, already coming near, also looking at me very intently, passes on.

Proceeding further, he turns around several times and looks again at me.

I take a risk and call after him in Armenian:

"Either I know you, or you know me!"

He stops, and looking at me, suddenly exclaims, "Ah! Black Devil!" and walks back.

It was enough for me to hear his voice, and already I knew who he was. He was no other than my distant relative, the former police court interpreter.

I already knew that several years before he had been exiled to some place in the Transcaspian region, but to where I did not know.

And I also knew that the reason for his exile was that he had stolen the affections of the paramour of the chief of police.

Can you imagine my inner exultation at such a meeting?

I will not describe how and about what we talked, while sitting on that terrace of the small *chaikhana* and continuing to drink green tea.

I will only say that on the following morning this distant relative of mine, the former police official, came to me accompanied by his friend, a police lieutenant.

From them I learned, first, that nothing serious threatened my companion.

He was arrested only because he was here for the first time, and nobody here had ever seen him before.

And as there were now many dangerous revolutionaries everywhere, he was arrested only in order to establish his identity.

This, they say, is not a complicated thing. They will write to the place where his passport was issued and order an inquiry into his political reliability; but if he must, in the meanwhile, disport himself with fleas and lice, what of it? To experience this is a very good thing as a preliminary education for the future life.

And secondly, added my distant relative, lowering his voice, your name appears on the list of sources disturbing for the peace of visitors to "Montmartre," places of frivolous amusement.

On this account, and also because of some other considerations, I, still in a very sick condition, decided to leave this place also as quickly as possible. For I could do nothing to help my friend.

Now entirely alone, and moreover with very limited funds, I set out in the direction of Central Asia.

After overcoming with unimaginable difficulties every kind of great and small obstacle, I came to the city of Yangihissar in the former Chinese Turkestan, where, from old friends of mine, I supplied myself with money and then found myself in that same place where I had lived several years before, while recovering my health when it had been shattered because of stray bullet number two.

This place is located on the southwestern edge of the Gobi Desert and represents to my mind the most fertile of all the parts of the surface of our earth.

And concerning the air of this place and its salutary influence on everyone inhaling it, I will say that it is truly purgatorial.

If in reality there exist paradise and hell, and if from them arises any radiation, then the air in the space between these two sources would surely have to be similar to this.

For on one side is a soil which almost literally pours from itself, as from a cornucopia, all kinds of earthly flora, fauna and phoscalia, and right next to this fertile soil is an area of many thousands of square kilometers representing literally hell, where not only nothing crops up but anything originating elsewhere that happens to get in its midst, is destroyed in a very short time, leaving no trace.

Namely, here on this small singular piece of the hard surface of our Earth the air of which, that is, our second food, originates and is transformed between the forces of paradise and hell, in me there had proceeded at the end of my first visit there, then also in an almost delirious condition, just that same self-reasoning concerning which, in my consciousness, on the evening of November 6th, as I have mentioned above, there flashed an idea which appeared to me then entirely absurd.

The first time, my friends brought me here in an unconscious condition, soon after I had been wounded by the second stray bullet.

At the beginning, near me were many friends among whom were also the five mentioned physicians.

And when, after the return of consciousness, I began to improve, all of them gradually went away, and I remained there with only one Tibetan and one very young Kara-Kirghiz.

Living there, far from people of all sorts, attended by these two sympathetic people who treated me almost maternally, and all the time nourished by the above-mentioned "cleansing air," I, within six weeks, recovered so that I already wished and was able at any moment to leave this salutary place.

Everything was already gathered and packed, and we awaited the coming of the young Kara-Kirghiz' father, with his three camels, in order to proceed on the journey.

As I had information that in one of the valleys of the mountain, then called "the peak of Alexander III," there were at that time several Russian officers, topographers of the Turkestan Topographical Administration, among whom was one of my very good friends, I intended first to go to them, and from there to join some large caravan and travel first to Andijan, then to the Transcaucasian region to see my relatives.

I was by that time, though not yet entirely, as it is said, "strong on my feet," and already feeling quite well.

It was night; the full moon was out. Thinking along paths of current associations, unnoticeably my thoughts passed again to the question which by this time had become finally transformed into the *idee fixe* of my inner world.

Continuing to think about this under the influence, from one side of a distant hollow din formed from sounds of milliards of lives of all possible outer forms and, from the other side, of an awesome silence, in me gradually rose in relation to myself a critical faculty of unprecedented strength.

At the beginning there were recollected in me all my blunders in my former searches.

While from one side I constated my blunders and in general the imperfections of the methods previously applied by me, from the other side it became clear how I ought to have acted in this or that instance.

I remember very well how my strength waned from these tense thoughts and, during this, some part of me time and again ordered me to get up quickly and rouse myself in order to stop such thoughts, but this I could not do, so strongly had I been involved in these same thoughts.

I don't know with what this would have ended if at the moment when instinctively I began to feel that I must lose consciousness, the three camels near me had not sat down.

At this I came to myself and got up.

By this time day was already dawning. Awake also were my young companions, who were already busying themselves with the usual preparations for morning life in the desert.

After talking with the old man, we decided to take advantage of the moonlight and set out in the evenings. Moreover, the camels could rest well during the day.

Instead of lying down to sleep awhile, I took with me a rifle and a traveling pail made of canvas and went to a nearby spring of very cold water on the very edge of the desert.

Undressing, I began very slowly to pour this cold water over me.

After this, though I felt quite well mentally, physically I became so weak that after dressing I was compelled to lie down there near the spring.

And then, being so weak physically and very well refreshed mentally, there proceeded in me that same self-reasoning, the essence of which became impressed in my consciousness forever and concerning which, on the evening of November 6th, 1927, flashed the mentioned idea.

Due to its remoteness, I do not remember the exact words of that first self-reasoning so discordant with my usual general state.

But, having preserved in myself the, so to say, "taste" of it, I can recollect it exactly, though in different words. It consisted of the following:

> Judging by my fitness during the last few days, it seems I again have come to life and willy-nilly will have to drag on and drudge as before.

> My God! Is it possible that I will have to experience again all that I lived through during periods of my fully collected active state, for the half-year before this last misfortune of mine?

> Not only to experience feelings alternating, almost regularly, between remorse for the inner and outer manifestations of my ordinary waking state, and loneliness, disappointment, satiety, and the rest, but primarily to be everywhere haunted by the fear of "inner emptiness"?

> What also have I not done, what resources have I not exhausted in my determination to reach a state where the functioning of my psyche in my usual waking state would flow in accordance with the previous instructions of my active consciousness, but all in vain!

In my past life, being forever merciless to my natural weaknesses, and almost all the time jealously keeping watch over myself, I could attain almost anything within the limits of man's possibilities, and in some fields attained even to such a degree of power as not one man, perhaps not even in any past epoch, had ever attained.

For instance, the development of the power of my thoughts had been brought to such a level that by only a few hours of self-preparation I could from a distance of tens of miles kill a yak.

or, in twenty-four hours, could accumulate life forces of such compactness that I could in five minutes put to sleep an elephant.

At the same time, in spite of all my desires and endeavors, I could not succeed in "remembering myself in the process of my general common life with others so as to be able to manifest myself, not according to my nature but according to the previous instructions of my "collected consciousness."

I could not attain the state of "remembering myself even sufficiently to hinder the associations flowing in me automatically from certain undesirable hereditary factors of my nature.

As soon as the accumulation of energy which enabled me to be in an active state was exhausted, at once associations of both thoughts and feelings began to flow in the direction of objects diametrically opposite to the ideals of my consciousness.

When I found myself in a state of complete dissatisfaction with food and sex, the leading factor of these associations of mine appeared to be primarily vindictiveness and, in a state of full satisfaction, they proceeded on a theme of the forthcoming pleasure of a meal and sex or of the gratification of self-love, vanity, pride, jealousy and other passions.

I thought deeply myself and tried to find out from others about the reasons for such a terrible situation within my inner world but could not clarify anything at all.

From one side it is clear that it is necessary to "remember myself" during the process of ordinary life also, and from the other side that there is a necessity for the presence of attentiveness, which is able to merge, in case of contact, with others.

Though in my past life I had tried everything, even had worn reminding factors of all kinds on my person, nothing helped. Perhaps these did help a little, while I carried them on me, but if so, it was only at the beginning, as soon as I stopped carrying them or got used to them, in a moment it was as if before.

There is no way out whatsoever. . ..

However, there is; there is one exit only to have outside myself, so to say, a "never-sleeping-regulating-factor."

Namely, a factor which would remind me always, in my every common state, to "remember myself."

But what is this!!! Can it be really so??!! A new thought!!!

Why hitherto could there not have come to my head such a simple thought?

Did I have to suffer and despair so much in order only now to think of such a possibility? . . .

Why could I not, in this instance also, look to a "universal analogy"?

And here also is God!!! Again God! . . .

Only He is everywhere and with Him everything is connected.

I am a man, and as such I am, in contrast to all other outer forms of animal life, created by Him in His image!!!

For He is God and therefore I also have within myself all the possibilities and impossibilities that He has.

The difference between Him and myself? must lie only in scale.

For He is God of all the presences in the universe! It follows that I also have to be God of some kind, of presence on my scale.

He is God and I am God! Whatever possibilities He has in relation to the presences of the universe, such possibilities, and impossibilities I should also have in relation to the world subordinate to me.

He is God of all the world, and also of my outer world.

I am God also, although only of my inner world. He is God and I am God!

For all and in everything we have the same possibilities and impossibilities!

Whatever is possible or impossible in the sphere of His great world should be possible or impossible in the sphere of my small world.

This is as clear as that after the night must inevitably come the day.

But how could I have failed to notice such a startling analogy?

I had thought so much about world creation and world maintenance, and in general about God and His deeds; and also, had discoursed with many others about all these matters; but never once had there come to my mind this simple thought.

And yet, it could not be otherwise.

Everything, without exception, all sound logic as well as all historical data, reveal and affirm that God represents absolute goodness; He is all-loving and all-forgiving. He is the just pacifier of all that exists.

At the same time why should He, being as He is, send away from Himself one of His nearest, by Him animated, beloved sons, only for the "way of pride" proper to any young and still incompletely formed individual, and bestow upon him a force equal but opposite to His own? . . . I refer to the "Devil."

This idea illuminated the condition of my inner world like the sun and rendered it obvious that in the great world for the possibility of harmonious construction there was inevitably required some kind of continuous perpetuation of the reminding factor.

For this reason, our Maker Himself, in the name of all that He had created, was compelled to place one of His beloved sons in such an, in the objective sense, invidious situation.

Therefore, I also have now for my small inner world to create out of myself, from some factor beloved by me, an alike unending source.

There arises now a question like this:

What is there contained in my general presence which, if I should remove it from myself, would always in my various general states be reminding me of itself?

Thinking and thinking, I came to the conclusion that if I should intentionally stop utilizing the exceptional power in my possession which had been developed by me consciously in my common life with people, then there must be forced out of me such a reminding source.

Namely, the power based upon strength in the field of "hanbledzoin," or, as it would be called by others, the power of telepathy and hypnotism.

Thanks mainly to this my inherency, developed in me by myself, /, in the process of general life, especially for the last two years, had been spoiled and depraved to the core, so that most likely this would remain for all my life.

And so, if consciously I would deprive myself of this grace of my inherency, then undoubtedly always and in everything its absence would be felt.

I take an oath to remember never to make use of this inherency of mine and thereby to deprive myself from satisfying most of my vices. In the process of living together with others, this beloved inherency will always be a reminder for me.

Never so long as I live shall I forget what state of mine resulted then, when, on the last day of my presence in that place, there happened the above-given self-reasoning which terminated in the conclusion which I have given above.

As soon as I realized the sense of this idea, I was as if reincarnated; I got up and began to run around the spring, without knowing what I was doing, like a young calf.

It all ended thus, that I decided to take an oath before my own essence, in a state of mind known to me, never again to make use of this property of mine.

I must also mention that, when I took the oath not to apply in life this inherency of mine, I made a reservation that my oath should not concern the application of it for scientific purposes.

For instance, I was very much interested then, and even now my interest has not entirely vanished, in increasing the visibility of distant cosmic centers many thousand times through the use of a medium, and in the cure of cancer by the power of suggestion.

All this was about two years prior to this my second sojourn here.

Toward the end of this second sojourn, in my being, the basic aim of almost all my life split into two definite aspects; and this time also thanks to my unhindered free mentation, that is, mentation which proceeded without the effects of the automatic influences of other people.

The trouble is that until this time the aim of my inner world had been concentrated only on my one unconquerable desire to investigate from all sides, and to understand, the exact significance and purpose of the life of man.

Until this time in my life, every activity into which I had rushed, every failure or success, had been connected with this sole aim of my inner world.

Even my propensity during this period for always traveling and trying to place myself wherever in the process of the mutual existence of people there proceeded sharp energetic events, such as civil war, revolutions, etc., had sprung also from this, my sole aim.

In the first place, during such events I had collected material for clearing up the problems of my principal aim in a more concentrated form and therefore more productively.

Secondly, as a result of the memory in my automatic mentation of the sight of all sorts of terrors flowing from the violent events which I had witnessed, and finally from accumulated impressions arising from conversations with various revolutionaries in the previous several years, first in Italy and then in Switzerland, and still more recently in Transcaucasia, there had crystallized in me little by little, besides the previous unique aim, another also unconquerable aim.

This other newly arisen aim of my inner world was summed up in this: that I must discover, at all costs, some manner or means for destroying in people the predilection for suggestibility which causes them to fall easily under the influence of "mass hypnosis."

And so, after this mentioned "regeneration" of the purpose of my inner world, while there continued the process of the recovery of my health, I composed in my thoughts a preliminary plan for my further activities.

So the idea which flashed into my consciousness on the evening of

November 6th consisted of the following:

In all probability my experience, during the last few days, of horrible despair and the unusually intense struggle of inner forces, which expressed itself this morning in an almost delirious self-reasoning, is really nothing else than the direct outcome of the self-reasoning that transpired in me when in an almost similar state, about thirty years ago, on the edge of the

Gobi Desert.

So, when I had more or less recovered, I began just from here to continue my research, but now for two definite aims instead of only one.

Here I will not write about what I undertook in continuation nor of how

I satisfied my inner "two-headed worm of inquisitiveness," as about this I have already written in enough detail in one of the books of this third series of my writings.

On this occasion I will say only that, after some years, I found it necessary to originate somewhere an institution for the preparation of "helper-instructors," in order to be able to put into the lives of people what I had already learned.

When this need arose, then, after all kinds of "comparative mentation," I selected Russia as most appropriate for this purpose.

With this aim I found myself in 1912 in the heart of Russia, the city of Moscow, where at once I started to organize such an institution under the name of "The Institute for the Harmonious Development of Man."

After two years of constant psychophysically tense work this organization was rapidly nearing completion when suddenly war broke out, a war which no one expected would continue long but which gradually became chronic and is now called "the World War."

Years dragged on; years which now already not only continued ceaselessly to demand tense activity from this ill-fated physical body of mine but sucked from it several times each day every kind of accumulated force for will and patience.

I was already beginning, strange as it may seem, to become adapted to the conditions created by this common evil of humanity, when suddenly, very s-l-o-w-l-y and very u-n-o-b-t-r-u-s-i-v-e-l-y there emerged Madame Russian Revolution.

This highly esteemed lady, though not yet standing firmly on her feet, at once began to sow within this poor physical body of mine such injuries and consequences that soon every atom of it cringed and could not get even one moment's peace.

The months flowed slowly by; it seemed that centuries passed.

my outer world already began to gasp for breath; at the same time, nevertheless, the vivification produced by the ever-opposing factors in my inner world increased to the highest degree.

In this state of inner vividity, without thinking about future prospects, I went into action.

Here began once more for this physical body of mine a series of "jugglings," unusual for the physique of man.

I started immediately on a journey, again through impassable places, this time in the mountains of the Caucasus, encountering, of course, as usually occurs on such journeys, frequent hunger and cold, added to which was continual anxiety about my near people, both those who had remained in the chaos behind and those present with me. Then, on the one hand, there began a dysentery in an aggravated form, and on the other hand there recurred an old illness called "zhaba" (*angina pectoris*) which had been considered entirely cured.

After this, several months of life under rough conditions, and then journeys from one country to another, with, aside from other things, the still inescapable necessity of being continually "on guard" so that neither I nor any one of the young men accompanying me, who as yet had not tasted the "delicacies" of human life, should fall victim to the at this time-common European "political psychosis."

Later: two years of ceaseless psychophysical activity for the organization of the Institute, this time in France.

At this point, in my long and unusual life, capricious and self-willed fate played me a mean trick.

By this time, it had already become clear, on the one hand, that without exception all I had had in the way of material resources in the country of former Russia had disappeared forever, and, on the other, that if within three months I did not have at least one "cool" million francs, I would go up the chimney, also forever.

And in this ill-fated physical body of mine, fatigued already to the limit, particularly by the last two years of strenuous work, because of these two "surprises" my mentation increased to such proportions that there was scarcely enough room for it in my cerebral cavity.

By some miracle or other my skull did not crack, and consequently, I decided to undertake a risky trip to America with many people among whom most, like myself, knew not one word of the local language, and no one had a penny in his pocket.

And then, to conclude all this, as a final chord, this battered physical body of mine which already had in its presence from its past life the previously enumerated marks together with an automobile going at a speed of 90 kilometers per hour crashed into a very thick tree one month after my return to Europe from America.

From such a "promenade," it was discovered I was not yet completely destroyed, and several months later, to my misfortune, into my totally mutilated body there returned in full force, with all its former attributes, my consciousness.

After this very soon there definitely emerged and became clear the two following unmistakable facts:

The first fact consisted in that all that I had finally more or less duly prepared in the last three years as a means for the possibility of achieving the second principal aim of my inner world must, due to a long pause in my personal participation, inevitably perish.

The second consisted in that, if the damage to my physical body which was caused by the automobile accident could be repaired, it would not, in any case, be at all soon.

When these two indubitable facts became quite clear to me, there began in me, within the already enveloping sphere of physical sufferings, moral sufferings also.

By this time, I could already move about the house and even ride in an automobile, of course always aided by someone.

Trying to be outwardly calm in everything, so as not to make my near people solicitous about me, I, inwardly, to the accompaniment of these two kinds of sufferings, thought and thought and thought about my situation.

During just these thoughts there arose in me a second series of moral sufferings.

Namely: I became aware, and after some days of unnoticed observation definitely established the fact, that the terrible illness of my sincerely loved wife, owing to the pause in my special treatment and also to her forgetfulness of self in ministering to me during my illness, had been so neglected that by this time there was already a question as to the possibility of curing her.

And in addition to this, the physicians treating my mother, who visited me as old friends, often mentioned to me that her chronic illness of the liver was becoming worse and worse.

I intentionally put away from me all thoughts about the reasons for this second series of moral sufferings, because I clearly understood my helplessness.

All my attention I intentionally concentrated on the causes of my first series of moral sufferings, and on bearing their consequences, in order not to experience the sufferings of the second series.

Just then, after many days of very active and serious mentation, I decided to utilize for my aim the only means open to me in my condition.

I decided to devote all the functions of my inner world to the end that somehow, I might expound the very essence of all the material elucidated by me for the welfare of humanity in the form of some kind of exposition.

With this decision, the very same day I set about dictating. This was January 1st, 1925.

I say "dictating" because at first, I was still so weak that I could not myself write but only dictate.

From this very moment, with physical sufferings and frequently also moral ones of the second series still continuing, I wrote and wrote, made changes, and wrote again.

From the very beginning, in order to clarify to myself the logical connection and successive development of the ideas of my exposition, I made it a custom in the evenings, both when home and when traveling, frequently to listen in the presence of others to the reading aloud of my current work.

These others were always either former pupils of the Institute founded by me who still remained with me, or simply old followers of my ideas from different countries whom I had accidentally met in my travels or who, in accordance with an old habit, continued periodically to visit me.

My situation at that time, as previously described, I constated and clearly elucidated for myself already in the month of September, and from then on, I frequently thought and thought about it, with the result that finally on the 6th of November I came to the categorical decision mentioned below.

So now, after everything which has been explained by me, I think already any reader can easily represent to himself what a dilemma then arose for me, when, after working for almost three years with unimaginable difficulties and being ready to die happily, I certainly and clearly understood, without doubt, that, of these writings of mine, people who did not know me personally could understand absolutely nothing.

My categorical decision, to which I came on the 6th of November 1927, consisted in the following:

To mobilize all the capacities and possibilities in my common presence, both those personally achieved and those inherited, and until the moment of the arrival of the next new year, which moment is that of my appearance on God's Earth, to discover some possible means of satisfactorily emerging from such a situation.

If unable to discover this means, then, on the evening of the last day of the old year, to begin to destroy all my writings, calculating the time so as, at midnight with the last page, to destroy myself also.

From that day on, while trying outwardly to live and work just as before so that my unusual state should not be noticed by the people surrounding me, I directed my thoughts only to this question of how to emerge from my desperate situation.

As my intentional mentation about this was very intense, in a day or two all the thoughts transpiring in me automatically began also to flow exclusively in connection with this question.

Time went on. . .. The Christmas holidays were nearing.

Engulfed introspectively at all times in such thought, I became perceptibly thinner and more feeble, and what's more, in addition to this, there for some reason began to reappear in me the consequences of my former ailments contracted many years before.

I remember very well that once during that period, while physically fagged to exhaustion because of a just-completed perilous descent in an automobile over a glacier pass in the Pyrenees, sitting in some provincial hole of a cafe, I put reproachfully to myself the following question:

"What now, exactly, will it be necessary for me to do so that first of all I myself may be completely satisfied with my writing and, secondly, that completely corresponding conditions may be created for its spreading?"

To this concrete question, I, after draining a great number of glasses of the local "delight" called Armagnac and after sufficiently long and serious mentation, formulated for myself the following answer:

Both of these completely satisfying wishes could be fulfilled only if there were actualized three definite aims.

First, that I rewrite anew all of my expositions, but in a new form which I now already understood.

Second, and parallel with this, that I study and from all sides make clear to myself the details of some of the, for me, still obscure and very deep questions concerning the common psyche of man and make use of this information in the development of my writings.

And third, that there may be the possibility during this period, while I am fulfilling all this, of renewing my physical body and my spirit to such a degree that, when my writings are completed, I can direct the spreading of them myself, with the energy and persistence which were peculiar to me in my youth.

That same day, while proceeding on my journey, and being absorbed in my fanciful thoughts, I calculated, by the way, that for the study of the mentioned obscure data of the common psyche of man and for the exposition of my writings in a new form there would be required not less than approximately seven years.

It will not be amiss to remark here that with regard to my estimate of the period of seven years there even arose in me a feeling of self-derision, and with such a feeling I thought the following:

Would it not be curious if I really lived for seven more years and finished during this period everything I have mentioned?

If this should in fact occur, then, in addition to everything else accomplished, I would be in possession of one or more excellent and extraordinary examples for a thoroughly practical proof of the law-conformably arising consequences resulting from the fundamental cosmic law of "sevenfold ness," which law is theoretically explained by me in sufficient detail in my writings.

The day before Christmas, I, being already very tired and worn out to the last degree thanks both to the continually active thinking and to the incessant driving in my automobile, returned to my home in Fontainebleau.

After getting out of the automobile I did not go at once to lie down in bed as I was accustomed to do but went instead into the garden with the hope that perhaps there in the quiet, and under the influence of familiar and cozy surroundings, I might relax a little.

Tottering a short distance down a pathway, I, because I was tired, sat down on the first bench I came to.

It happened that I sat on the very bench on which it had been my habit, during the first year of my writing, often to sit and work.

At that time there frequently used to come and sit down by me on this bench, on each side of me, two near beings, the only ones close to my inner world.

One of them always adored by me was my old mother and the other, my uniquely and sincerely beloved wife.

At the present time both of these women, uniquely nearest to my inner world, peacefully lie forever side by side in a cemetery which is for them as well as for me in an entirely strange country.

First to die, from a long-standing illness of the liver, was my mother; some months later, from the most terrible contemporary scourge, the disease cancer, went my wife.

This country France, by the way, which is the last resting place for those two beings uniquely nearest to me, but which is indeed absolutely foreign to my nature, remains in my feelings, thanks only to this, as if it were my native land.

And so, as I sat on this bench and almost mechanically observed the familiar surroundings, in me, by the association of ideas, there began to be recollected the different experiences I had had in this same place.

Suddenly remembering, I visualized as though in reality a picture which I had frequently seen during the short periods of rest from my active mentation.

Namely, a picture of how from my left, in the company of two peacocks, a cat and a dog, there slowly strolled down the path my unforgettable old mother.

At this point, it is impossible not to remark on the relation between my mother and the mentioned animals, as this was indeed unusual in the lives of contemporary people.

These four differently natured animals would already know in advance just when my mother was coming out, and, gathering near the door of her home, they would await her appearance and afterwards, wherever she went, would very "sedately" accompany her.

Always the cat would walk in front, the two peacocks at the sides and the dog behind.

Usually when my mother left her home, which was called "Le Paradou," and proceeded in my direction there would approach from the house called "Le Prieure," my wife.

Both walked with the help of a stick, and both were stooped.

It must be confessed that the bent figure of the first did not touch me so much, because I accounted and accepted this as the normal destiny of every person of esteemed age.

But to the bowed posture of the second I was quite unable to reconcile myself; each time when I noticed it there arose in me a feeling of revolt and my heart pounded like that of a balking horse.

For it was only a trifling eighteen years earlier that, thanks to this now stooped and sallow-faced woman and her accidental presence in the place where the awarding of prizes for beauty was going on in St. Petersburg, the famous Lena Cavalieri, then in the bloom of her youth, was deprived of the first prize.

Continuing to sit on the bench, and also continuing not to hinder the automatic flow of thoughts regarding those two dear-to-me women in connection with this place, I remembered and very strongly experienced in myself again that exact feeling of being deeply touched which I had more than once experienced when they spoke to each other.

I remembered how it often happened that they would sit by my side, one on my right and the other on my left, almost touching me, and so seated that, although very quiet in order not to hinder me, they would sometimes when I bent forward concentrating on my work whisper to each other behind my back.

And this whispering of theirs and their complete understanding of each other always caused in me this feeling of being deeply touched.

The fact is that my mother knew not one word of the language which my wife spoke and my wife in turn understood no word of the language which my mother spoke.

In spite of this, not only did they very freely interchange their ordinary opinions, but they had imparted to each other in a very short time all the peculiar experiences and the full biographies of their lives.

Because of the common object of this centrigravital love, there was soon fabricated by them a very peculiar independent dialect, consisting of many different languages.

My thoughts, while there still continued in me the experiencing of the mentioned feeling, unnoticed passed again to the theme torturing me during the last days' self-questioning.

Thinking again about this, I got up in order to go home, as it was already beginning to get considerably colder.

After several steps, in my thoughts there suddenly realized

itself, and after only a little confrontation there was established for me very clearly, the following:

During the period of my greatest occupation with writing, the quality of my labor-ability and its productivity was always the result of, and was dependent upon, the length and gravity of the constating with my active mentation of the automatic that is, passive experiencing's of suffering proceeding in me concerning these two, for me, nearest women.

For already from the very beginning, when I was physically quite helpless, I approached my writing feeling sure beyond a shadow of doubt of the hopelessness of their health and of their imminent deaths.

From then on, there began to happen this: as soon as my active mentation in regard to the writing question weakened a little, immediately all the spiritual parts of my presence began to associate in me only about them.

As every kind of association about them always entailed the process of suffering so I, in order not to experience this unpleasant process, immediately buried myself in the question of writing.

It is necessary here to confess that my sufferings were chiefly on behalf of my wife.

In this, as 1 now understand it, me so to say "implacable revolt" against the injustice of casual, self-willed destiny played a great part.

The trouble was that while I was considered by many people at that time (and perhaps even now still am, I don't know) the sole man on earth who could cure completely this illness of hers, nevertheless, at the given time, because of my own illness, I could not do this.

The aplomb which I manifested just now can be, if wished, justified, and adequately understood by every reader if he will read only one chapter from my writings on the subject of "the laws of vibrations."

And thus, with turbulent feelings and wild thoughts, swaying as if blind drunk, I somehow made my way from the park to my room.

There, without undressing, I lay down on my bed and, contrary to all habits, fell asleep immediately and slept through the whole night.

And the next morning, when I did awake, the constatation that I had made the previous night recalled itself.

I began once more to remember these things and to compare them.

And this time, beyond any doubt, I again established that during the first three years of my authorship, my labor-ability, as well as my productivity, in reality at all times strictly corresponded in its duration with the length and quality of the, so to say, "degree of contact" between my consciousness and the suffering proceeding in me on behalf of my mother and my wife.

My labor-ability at that time was indeed phenomenal, for I wrote and rewrote at least 10, 000 kilos of paper and touched upon almost all questions which could possibly arise in the mentation of man in general.

The establishment at this time, with a fresh mind, of such a fact perplexed me seriously.

It perplexed me seriously because I already knew, and had been convinced before without any doubt, thanks to my own manifold experience, that although it is possible to attain any self-imposed aim it can only be done exclusively through conscious suffering.

To explain my case, however, by such an objective possibility was utterly impossible.

And it was impossible to explain because in this particular case I suffered unconsciously, while this process proceeded in me automatically in accordance with my typicality and the accidental crystallization in it of corresponding psychic factors.

The interest that arose in my being this morning was of such strength that the "being-thirst" possessing me to find at any cost an exit from my difficult situation entirely disappeared, and in its place arose an unconquerable desire to learn the reason for this.

Namely, to learn why and in what manner my suffering in this instance could assist in the increase of my labor-ability.

The beneficent result for me from this "Inner-World Revolution" occurring within me was that from that moment on I could freely, without influence of partial feelings, again think in my habitual way.

The totality of such mentation of mine led to this, that, in the evening while watching the children around the Christmas tree and their unrestrained joy, there suddenly, as if by itself, came into existence in me a conviction of the full possibility of attaining all the three tasks indispensable for me, through the forces of the inner-world struggle.

Namely, those forces which arise in every person due to incessant friction between his consciousness and the automatic experiencing's of his nature.

I remember very well that because of my just-mentioned conviction my whole being was filled as if by some singular, never till now experienced, feeling of joy.

Simultaneously with this, in me of itself, and without any manipulation on my part, there appeared the sensation of so to say "self-remembering," also of a never-before-experienced vigor.

When the children's holiday was over, I immediately retreated to my room and locked myself in, of course making preliminary arrangements that coffee be amply supplied, and began to think of what was to be done further.

Just that same night, after a prolonged comparison of thoughts, I decided the following:

From the very beginning, from the 1st of January, to begin to work out anew all that I had conceived for exposition, devoting to it only one half of my waking state.

And to devote the second half of the whole time of my waking state, until April 23rd, which is my name day, exclusively to the illumination of possible ways of procedure, and to the formulation of an approximate plan for later sequential fulfillment.

Beginning with the 1st of January, I began to work not all day long as before, but only at definite hours of the morning and of the evening, devoting the rest of the time either to writing letters of inquiry to some of my friends whom I respect, or to thinking and working out in my mind different details of the general program, on the basis of everything I had already clarified, as well as in terms of psychological and physiological laws known to me.

The different conclusions I arrived at during these mentation's in the two weeks that followed brought me to the point where I decided not to make a detailed program for all my future outer life but to make one every three months.

Once every three months I was to bring myself into an "all-centers-balanced" state, as it is called, and in this state, in accordance with the surrounding conditions of life existing at that time, and also those that might arise in accordance with the theory of probabilities, to make a program in full detail for the succeeding three months.

On the eve of my name day, in accordance with all the deductions made by me during this time, and also thanks to some wise advice from one of my oldest friends, a very respected person, I finally resolved the following:

Parallel with the fulfillment of the detailed program which would be composed by me every three months, from my name day on to carry out into life infallibly, to sequential fulfillment, the three following tasks:

First: always, in the beginning of the realization as well as several times during the action, to stimulate artificially within myself the three following impulses:

For the first aim, that is, for writing, to rouse within myself the impulse of "persistence"; for the second, that is, for the study of the deep-rooted minutiae of the common psyche of man, the impulse of "patience"; and for the third, that is, for the renewal of my organism, the "suffering" resulting from automatic experiencing's.

Second: whomever I should meet, for business, commerce, or any other purpose, whether an old or new acquaintance, and whatever his social standing might be, I had immediately to discover his "most sensitive corn" and "press" it rather hard.

And third: not to refuse anything to my physical body, especially insofar as food is concerned; at the same time always, after satisfying myself and during digestion, to stimulate within myself for not less than fifteen minutes the feeling of pity, thinking of other people who had no means of having such food.

These three just enumerated "will-tasks," which, it is timely to mention, served as guiding origins for all my intentional activities, were combined by me in order to achieve simultaneously several absolutely different aims.

Although these three different aims will also be clarified along with others in the following text of the book, I wish to say already here, that, in their composition, the constatation in my mentation of one small fact played a large part.

Namely, once during my reflections about the construction and functioning of the nervous system of man, I, by the way, remembered and, thinking further, very definitely established the following:

During the second period of me so to say "Great Illness" after the automobile accident, that is, when my consciousness returned, while my body was still helpless, and when I was visited by different friends, then, no matter whether they talked to me or just remained about, for several hours after their departure I felt very badly.

Their sincere sympathy in reality gave birth in me every time to thoughts which may be expressed as follows: "came, sucked me out like vampires and went away."

So, having decided on this program, I, before beginning the realization in practice of everything thought out by me for unfailing fulfillment, took an oath before my own essence.

This was on the night of May 6th, 1928, new calendar.

After the so to say, "simultaneous pacification of numerous tapeworms," usual in my house on this day, I again locked myself in my room, and at this time, having brought myself into a suitable state, took for this case my first, solemn vow.

It will be advisable to mention here, by the way, that on this name day of mine, because of a certain action toward me on the part of one of the people near me, I decided to realize the following:

In the future, under the pretext of different worthy reasons, to remove from my eyesight all those who by this or that make my life too comfortable.

During these seven years, I, in order to make possible the attainment of my then composed aims, infallibly carried out in the sphere of my inner as well as outer world a great number of peculiar "will-tasks" of different durations.

I imposed them, changed, rechanged, or dropped them altogether, always in accord, on the one hand, with the already arisen or expected circumstances of my ordinary life, and on the other hand with the arising in me, in connection with writing, of new ideas and new desires for the future.

Today is the 2nd of April 1935, new calendar; and the final time limit for the intentional introducing by me into life of all the self-imposed aims and "will-tasks" for the possibility of attainment of the three mentioned fundamental aims will come on the 23rd of April of this same year, old calendar.

During this period, because of my "scatterbrained trick," really unusual in the life of people, I accomplished more than satisfactorily the following:

First, "puffed" three small booklets into ten substantial volumes.

Second, not only understood from all sides different deep-rooted minutiae of the common psyche of man, suspected by me and intriguing me all my life, but constated unexpectedly many such "delicacies," which, had they been known to Mr. Beelzebub, would, I daresay, grow the horns mentioned by me in the next to the last chapter of the first series of my writings, even on his hooves.

Third, my health is now in such condition that I not only, as you may see, live, and write such an already ultra-fantastic book, but intend to outlive all my past, present and future conscious enemies.

All three of the aims, self-imposed seven years ago, I daresay I had already achieved last year, but I decided to continue the fulfillment of different "will-tasks" until the expiration of the seven-year period, because of the three following reasons:

First, last year I was not entirely satisfied with the degree of achievement of my third fundamental aim; namely, during changes of weather, I still felt rather serious rheumatic pains.

The second reason consisted in this, that, because of the occurrence in these present years of the periodic maximum operation, in relation to the earth, of the cosmic law "solioo-nensius," I found the publication of my writings still untimely.

I consider it necessary here, concerning the cosmic law just mentioned, to say the following:

Of the name alone of such a law, I happened to learn for the first time, when still very young, from a certain very ancient Armenian papyrus, and the details of this law I accidentally cleared up many years later, during my study of the so-called "map of pre-sand Egypt" which had come, also altogether accidentally, into my possession.

To odds and ends out of the totality of what I cleared up about the law of "solioo-nensius," I referred, it seems, in the second book of the first series of my writings, in the chapter entitled "Russia."

And as to the third reason, it is necessary for its elucidation to say first the following:

This book which I am now writing (was originally intended to be) the last book of the third series of my writings, which will be published. The first was begun and finished, in a form entirely satisfactory to me, already long ago.

On this book, I set to work at the end of the third year of my literary activity and, working at it only at intervals, completed it in three years. Notwithstanding the fact that for the writing of such a, as it might be called, "summarizing-concluding" book I had to put in a great deal of labor, unpleasant experiences, and money, etc., I was nevertheless compelled, almost on the very day when I finally completed it, to destroy in its entirety all this, my tedious work of many years.

I was compelled to destroy not only this book itself but also everything prepared for the affirmation of the spirit of its essence.

During just that period, when I was finishing the writing of this "concluding" book, the functioning of both my usual mentation's, that is, active and passive, proceeded tensely with unusual intensity.

With my active mentation, I was putting the so to say "last polish" on the contents of this book so important for the whole totality of my writings, and the passive was occupied with the transformation of that same material which more than anything else has assisted me in having, at the present time, ideal health.

So just then, while fulfilling in constant intensity of mentation my various will-tasks, I began to notice in my own inner world as well as in others many particularities previously unknown to me.

And when I began for my own conviction to check statistically these unexpectedly noticed particularities and to establish the fact of their actuality, then I found all that I had written in this last book entirely worthless for my premeditated aim.

So, thanks to this, the third reason thus consisted in this, that it was necessary for this predetermined aim to write a new book with an entirely new content.

Having just written about publishing this book, I must now, willy-nilly, say something concerning one certain measure applied by me for the possibility of attaining the aims set myself which, to explain clearly, would require my bringing in here and citing all the following:

I would have to cite all verbal formulations for the particularities and laws which recently have become known to contemporary people through, as they are called, "radiography," "telepathy," "telepesi" and to bring, in its entirety, the whole science of white and black magic.

As it is utterly impossible to do this, I shall therefore limit myself to saying the following:

Three years ago, when there had simultaneously arisen three very serious facts hindering my work and insuperable by usual means, I then, among other measures unusual in the life of people, for the purpose of conquering these "uninvited guests," also wrote one small booklet under the title *The Herald of Coming Good.*

This I wrote especially for certain people who had already long been considered followers of my ideas or, during the existence of the Institute founded by me, had been pupils in one or another of its branches.

This booklet was printed in nine languages, a thousand copies in each language.

Although every measure was then taken to prevent its falling into the hands of people who as yet did not know me, this was not entirely achieved, and now, to the number of several hundred copies, it is unfortunately, as it is said, "passing from hand to hand."

And so, having this in mind, I consider it my duty, for the possibility of attaining my third fundamental aim also to entire satisfaction, to give here the following advice:

If you as yet have not read this book entitled *The Herald of Coming Good*, then thank the circumstance and do not read it.

Just here it will not be amiss to also say that for the possibility of attaining my third fundamental aim, also to entire satisfaction, I for the past year even ceased to write.

Not only intentionally ceased writing but even, for the past year, have always insofar as possible, of course with a very great inner struggle, not admitted the proceeding in me of any active mentation.

I resorted to such a really "barbarous" measure in order that the automatically experienced sufferings proceeding in me, by means of which chiefly I have achieved this aim of mine, should be actualized in me more productively.

Even my last journey to America was made chiefly for the purpose of obtaining this productivity.

And this was in consequence of the fact that after the terrible automobile accident which happened to me, I mingled only with Americans, and therefore almost all of my acquaintances of the last decade are there, and in view of this I could, without resorting to any special measures, always very easily have at my disposal fertile soil of all kinds and degrees of vivifying-ness for the sowing of Divine seeds for the germination of beneficent factors for my being.

Although all the strange will-tasks and original principles which I have applied to life during the last seven years are, as already stated, elucidated in the subsequent text of this book, yet the feelings of admiration and gratitude overflowing in me bid the whole of me here, in the initial chapter, to comment on that principle of mine for outer life which unexpectedly became for me, so to say, the "inexhaustible source."

I refer to that already-mentioned principle which I characterized by the words "to press the most sensitive corn of everyone I met."

Thanks to this principle, which turned out to be miracle-working for me, I, besides having always and everywhere an abundance of material for my chief aim, that is, for my regeneration, also, thanks only to it, so affected everyone who met me, that he himself, without any effort on my part whatsoever, as if with great satisfaction and complete readiness, took off his mask presented to him with great solemnity by his papa and mama; and thanks to this I at once acquired an unprecedentedly easy possibility of unhurriedly and quietly feasting my eyes on what his inner world contained, not only of the accidentally surviving worthy data proper to man, but also of all the nauseating filth accumulated from his absolutely abnormal so-called "education."

This, and only this, for me Divine principle, enabled me to discern and understand at last those deeply hidden nuances of the human soul that had intrigued me all my life.

To it, and to it alone, am I indebted for all that I now possess.

And I possess such "inner wealth" that in the objective sense it is worth many times more than all the money that can be imagined by the human brain, such as, for example, the whole estate which fell to the so-called "New York five and ten heiress," plus all the money hoarded in cash by the peasants of France.

However, concerning the significance and the value of the inner wealth acquired by me, I will also explain in detail at the end of this last book.

Meanwhile, in order to acclaim this principle, I shall say that on account of it I lost all without exception that I possessed of what people call wealth.

Because of it I lost not only the wealth that I possessed but also all so-called "friends," and even the so to say "privilege of being envied" in a word, all that because of which only I was several years ago considered by a great many people no mere "dog's tail" but one of the first ranking "aces" of contemporary life.

In spite of all this, I, today, when I write these lines and when the surrounding conditions of my ordinary life grown law-abidingly worse and worse because of my inflexible carrying out in life of the tasks set myself, and among them this principle of mine are already so far gone that I cannot even imagine how I shall pull through, bless this principle with all my being.

About the circumstances of ordinary life which have today resulted for me, I shall without fail explain also at the end of this book, if, of course, I succeed in somehow carrying on for one more month.

And I shall then explain, also, why I used the expression "grown law-abidingly worse."

I shall without fail explain it, for in all this there is not only much that is instructive but also such comicality that, if all the wits got together purposely to think it up, they could not think up even the tenth part of it.

Having expressed my gratitude to this principle for the acquisition of inner riches, I must now be quite impartial and put the question squarely. ... Is this so?

Could this principle invented by me be also, in all other

surrounding conditions of ordinary life, such a vivifying factor?

Frankly speaking, according to the opinion of my subconscious, I must say. . .. no.

This could have happened only thanks to the general material crisis.

I must therefore express my thanks to such a general human misfortune.

Since it would be rather awkward to do that, I shall therefore retain my former opinion.

Now, while expressing half-mockingly my gratitude to this uncertain factor for the inner riches which I now possess, I remembered many living people near to me, who, because of my mentioned egoistic ideas, must have had many disappointments.

Among such people, who willingly or unwillingly did not have a very "sweet" life, there were many really near to me in blood as well as in spirit.

In concluding this chapter of the third series of my writings, I, almost on the eve of the sequential fulfillment of my egoistical aims, addressing all those near to me, shall speak only about two "substantial factors," formed in my inner world.

The first, formed in my being while yet in childhood, and which is the sovereign of my convictions, may be formulated as follows: "Only then may a man be a good altruist to his nearest, when at times he can be a complete egoist."

And the second was formed within me two years after I began to actualize the three aims of my seven-year task.

While working intensively on the books intended for publication, under conditions of law abidingly arisen misfortunes, I, when

I noticed that because of my pursuit of my egoistical ideas those near me were becoming worse and worse, once brought myself into a state of mind by a technique I acquired from my father, and through self-suggestion crystallized in my presence this psychic factor, in terms of the following supposition:

If I should attain my self-imposed aims, and should still survive, then I would live with a definite program, as follows:

one third of all my waking state I shall devote to pleasures of my own body; the second third, exclusively to those by that time remaining near to me, in spirit as well as in blood; and the third part to science, that is, to all humanity.

Thus now, after everything that has been clarified in this introductory chapter, I advise, and at that very sincerely, all my readers, both those who know me and those who do not, and also all my dear friends and not less dear "enemies," to try to understand properly the essence of the text of this, my last book, and especially the essence of the concluding chapter.

The concluding chapter of my final book I intend to name "The Inner and Outer World of Man" and to explain in it a question, unusual in the mentation of people, but nevertheless the most preeminent of all questions, from the totality of which follow almost all the misunderstandings of our common lives.

Very sincerely I advise you to understand it because, if nothing else, the common presence of everyone will acquire a perhaps even subconsciously acting "factor-pacifier" for the larger part of the futile worries and moral sufferings occurring in their lives.

Above I used the word "enemies" not casually but because, first, the very best friends for my real self, that is, for my inner world, appear, strange as it may seem, to be some from among a great number of my "staunch enemies," at the present time scattered all over the world; and because, second, it may serve me ideally as a good example for the concluding chapter of the present book, and therefore I shall use it as such.

Recollecting now through association some of such "enemies" especially dear to my inner world, I, feeling sincerely touched, wish, already here in this introductory chapter of my last book, for their pleasure or displeasure, to quote a few from among the sayings known to me, sayings of popular wisdom which have reached our days through "legomonisms" from the ancient days.

I said for their pleasure or displeasure because I do not know which current of life's river they follow at present.

Since then, much time has elapsed. . .. Whether they have remained in that current of life's river into which I, unmerciful to myself, had directed them just that current which sooner or later must fall into the fathomless ocean, I do not know; or whether the temptations of life, likewise law-abiding, have pushed them into the current which sooner or later must fall into the abyss, for further involution and evolution.

And so, the first of these sayings of popular wisdom runs as follows:

"A man is not a pig to forget good, nor is he a cat to remember evil:"

"The first refusal to a person who is devoid of conscience or consideration will destroy the results of even thousands of good deeds formerly manifested toward him by you:"

"Only that person is worthy to be a follower of any religion who, although he remembers the wrong done to him by someone, will not manifest any evil toward him:"

"You will be reasonable only then when you will learn to distinguish your future good or evil from that of your present"

"Such is the nature of man, that for your first gift, he prostrates himself.

for your second kisses your hand,

for the third fawns,

for the fourth, just nods his head once,

for the fifth, becomes too familiar,

for the sixth, insults you,

and for the seventh, sues you because he was not given enough:"

———————————————————————

INTRODUCTION

November 6th, 1934
Childs Restaurant
Columbus Circle
New York

While I, as may be said, "groaned" and "puffed" over the last chapter of the third book of the second series of my writings, in the process of my "subconscious mentation," that is to say, in my automatically flowing thoughts, the center of gravity of interest was concentrated by itself on the question: how should I begin the third series of books predetermined by me for writing, namely, that series of books which according to my conviction was destined to become in a short time so to say "edifyingly instructive" for all the creatures of Our Common Father similar to myself; but here I must sincerely confess that soon after I had chosen for myself the profession of a writer, as the most corresponding to my unexpectedly arisen physical state, and when, parallel to the improvement in my physical state, I clearly understood that, thanks to my personal written explanations, a great benefit will arise for the majority of contemporary people as well as for future generations, I determined by this very series of books consciously to acquit myself with Great Nature for my arising and existence, chiefly for an existence not merely as an "ordinary life," automatically fulfilling some purpose necessary for the general realizations of Great Nature, but rather as an existence determinate and conscious, impartially evaluating itself and, in addition, gifted with the capacity of all-round perfecting and independent unity.

The outcome of these recent reflections, combined with my conscious thoughts of today upon finishing this last-mentioned book, brought me to the categorical decision to begin this "edifyingly instructive" series of books with the description of the events connected with my last two visits to some of the cities of North America, and to cite in concise form the talks delivered by me there to a certain group of the followers of my ideas which had already been organized ten years before during my first visit in New York.

I wish to begin with this description chiefly because upon these talks, as I planned them in my thoughts, a corresponding foundation may be built for everything which I have decided to introduce into the conscious life of people by means of this third and last series of my writings; furthermore, because the publication of these lectures, combined with the description of the events and causes which provoked them, to which events and causes I reacted by means of these very talks of definite form and sequence, will, I have almost no doubt, create in their totality as to say "automatically acting factor" for the possible saving from their total ruination of many thousand people of both sexes from various countries in Europe, Asia and America.

In this introductory book of the third series, I shall expose the "quintessence" of five talks, four of which were delivered by me at the end of 1930 and the beginning of 1931, and one other at the end of 1931 or the beginning of 1932.

For the readers of this series of my expositions, no matter in which degree of consciousness they may rank themselves, it would not in my opinion be superfluous to know, among other things, from which of my conceptions and instinctive suppositions was derived the phrase I used: "consciously to acquit myself with Great Nature."

This phrase burst forth from me almost involuntarily and took a shape which derived from the totality of my instinctive and conscious conviction that by this act of making known this last series of my writings, I could rely on fulfilling what is in my opinion the most important duty of a man who has reached responsible age, which consists in preparing without fail for the benefit of posterity, according to one's own individuality, certain profitable instructions; furthermore, I could by this same act, albeit quite subjectively, justify the sense of all my past intentional labors and conscious renunciations of all kinds of benefits which are generally crystallized in the life of contemporary people, and which have always been very easy for me to obtain; and finally, I hope, in the moment of my last breathing, to experience with no possible mental, sensitive or instinctive doubt the impulse, sacred for a man, which was called by the ancient Essenes "impartial self-satisfaction."

In order that there should arise in the mentation of the readers of this book, for a better orientation and an easier logical confrontation with what will follow, a "something" which existed on Earth before the Babylonian civilization in a branch of science named "Theomathos" and was called "a vivifying factor for objective assuming" I refer, of course, to the mentation of those readers who, as soon as they became acquainted with my expositions, were guided by and closely followed my advice, I wish first of all to try, for their inner sight, to depict by a verbal description various information, the totality of which might help them to represent in true perspective and clearly understand two situations which occurred in the process of my ordinary life during the time of my writing activity.

The first situation arose just at the beginning of my writing activity, after the motor accident, that great misfortune which occurred to me, when I liquidated everything connected with my previous forms of conscious activity for the welfare of those around me and began to write. From that time on I began particularly to avoid all kinds of meetings and to shun conversing with people who had somehow become aware of my ideas and also naturally wanted to speak to me in order to become better acquainted with them.

I took this measure from the very beginning of my writing activity in order not to receive or at least to receive in a smaller degree, the shocks upon my mental associations of those "rarefied" abstract questions, concerning which, in recent years, I had been obliged in my talks with various people to adapt myself to their different degrees of comprehension, acquiring thus in regard to these questions almost an automatic response. I wished generally not to take in the impressions of ordinary life, which were unnecessary for me, and could interfere with the established tempo of my mentation in this task I had voluntarily imposed upon myself.

To characterize my intentional "inner isolation" from those external impressions which hindered my writing activity, it will be enough to say that during this time I did not once read a newspaper or even hold one in my hand, and it was almost the same with letters and telegrams. I say "almost," because during this time I did read thirteen to fifteen letters and wrote about six or seven, in spite of having received, particularly in the first year, hundreds daily.

As the mention of such a free attitude toward my correspondence is a sort of confession of one of my secrets, slipped in involuntarily, I feel the need also to confess something else regarding the correspondence addressed to me. This would be in perfect accord with that fundamental principle of mine, always applied by me in ordinary life, and which is formulated by the words: *"If one is on a spree, one must not stop at trifles."* (See "The Arousing of Thought," *Beelzebub's* Tales to His Grandson.)

After my motor accident, already mentioned, making an exception only of the representatives of the French government, I closed the doors of my house to all people, both those who already knew me and those who had only heard about me and were curious to see me probably with the aim, as most of them believed, of finding out for themselves what I was like and what my ideas were. When in the second year I was especially "bombarded" with big piles of letters, I commissioned one of the people near me to open these letters without giving them to me, and if there were no what are called "enclosures" nor any indication of their immediate dispatch, to destroy them in such a way that not even their "astral smell" should remain in my house, but if there were enclosures, then, as I had the habit of expressing myself, according to the number of English, or at worst American, "zeros" adorning them, to act in the following way:

If one zero adorned the enclosure, then the letter was to be destroyed without residue and the enclosure given to the children living in my house for buying toys; if the enclosure had two zeros, the letter was to be given forthwith to my private secretary and the enclosure to the kitchen administration on duty in the Prieure and only those letters were to be handed to me personally which were adorned with three or more of the aforesaid zeros.

This arrangement of mine, by the way, still continues today, but in the near future, that is to say, the moment I finish this first book of the third series of my writings, I propose to change this arrangement in such a way that all the letters and telegrams without exception are to be destroyed and the enclosures with no fewer than four zeros, handed to me, those with three to my secretary, those with two to the children living in my house, and all the enclosures with one zero will be sent to the poor children of the towns of Fontainebleau and Avon.

Now that I have publicly confessed to such an unceremonious attitude not only toward my correspondence but also toward people, some of whom were at that time and perhaps still are considered in various European countries powerful and even "illustrious," it will be right to say that if my consciousness allowed my particular nature to manifest such a "boldness" and even to express it in written form, making it accessible to the perception of every two-legged breathing creature, in spite of his representing, in the sense of comprehension, some geometrical figure such as a "cube," "square," or "zigzag," it is because I have already succeeded in fulfilling the greatest part of the task I set myself, in spite of all kinds of obstructive factors both those which arose according to law and those engendered by various types amidst us who unfortunately bear also the name of "man" and who, as explained in a very ancient legend, arising and existing among us ordinary people, are usually formed by Nature in such a way that two results ensue: firstly, the cosmic substances transformed through them during their vegetation and not, as they themselves believe it, their life, serve as "cathode elements" for the maintenance on Earth of "objective Good" in the life of all humanity, and that, secondly, the elements composing their common presence are transformed after they perish to serve as a supplement to the used-up products for the requirements of Hell.

Speaking shortly, this attitude of mine in respect of meeting and conversing with all kinds of people became from the first year of my writing activity firmly established in the course of my external automatic life, and I tried not to change it until several months prior to my last journey to America: namely, when I had finished the exposition in its first draft of all the material which I had planned to write, the first series in its final form, the second in its first version and the third at least partly written.

The second of the facts I mentioned was that, while the acuteness of my memory in connection with the questions of writing had become sharpened during my writing activities to an extraordinary degree, so that, for instance, I always could and even now still can remember where, in which notebook out of many thousands I have filled up, and in what connection with another thought a particular thought is expressed and has to be repeated in a different form and precisely in what other place, and could and even still can remember on which of the already tens of thousands of pages of the notebooks I have filled up, in which sentence and in which word there were letters I automatically wrote strangely incorrectly, yet at the same time, during this period, when I unavoidably had to meet new people, there was scarcely a single meeting or even a single conversation which formerly would have unfailingly made an impression on me which made any impression at all on my memory; and even on the next day, when it was sometimes indispensable for me to remember it, I could not with all my desire and tenseness, remember anything at all about the meetings and conversations which had taken place only the day before.

But when, due to nearing the completion of my expositions, the intensity of my inner preoccupation with questions of writing had diminished, there was acquired in my nature, which happens to be formed in a particular way, the possibility of being able without experiencing a feeling similar to "remorse of conscience" to take an interest in life questions other than those relating to the task set to myself for the given period under a special oath made in a definite state which since childhood had been indicated and firmly instilled in me by my father. In this "psychic state," I undertook to put the final touches to the second series, continuing to work, of course, as before, that is to say, mostly traveling in various European countries, principally in France, and being occupied with writing exclusively in various public places, such as restaurants, cafés, "dance halls" and other kindred "temples" of contemporary morality.

When from this time on my relationship with all kinds of people was renewed, and I began observing them again, due to my half-released attention, with a particular capacity intentionally developed in my early youth and which consisted in "being able not to identify with the external manifestations of others," I began to notice and upon repeated meetings became more and more convinced that in the psyche of all of them, men and women alike, who had some knowledge of and interest in my ideas, especially in the psyche of those who had already begun to attempt to make in practice some experiments on themselves, supposed to correspond to my ideas, there proceeded something "wrong," so definitely "all wrong" that it was noticeable of course with a certain knowledge of observation even to every average person.

These repeated constatations not only began to alarm me but aroused gradually in my psyche the "needful thirst for knowledge," for the purpose of understanding the causes of this fact.

The result of this was that at subsequent meetings with such people I began, for the purpose of elucidation, to observe them particularly and by means of indirect questions to probe for more material which might enable me to understand the origin of this strange and, for me personally, sorrowful fact.

Each new meeting with such people, and even the associations provoked by recollection of this as yet inexplicable fact, on the one hand began to increase my interest and the thirst for knowledge to such a degree of manifestation that it became almost my idee fixe; on the other hand, the automatic thoughts about it began to hinder me seriously in my usual inner struggle with the lawful refusal of my nature to submit to my consciousness and interfered thus with the possibility of my full concentration on the continuation of my work, which demanded the greatest attention.

But when finally, at the end of 1930, 1 arrived in New York and on the first day I happened to find myself among a large number of Americans, followers of my ideas, and when I observed the same phenomenon also among them, then this produced such a deep impression on me, and the force of reaction was so strong, that it provoked a cold shivering similar to that which takes people who are afflicted by the so-called "yellow malaria of Kushka."

I then even, to "throw dust into their eyes," increased my usual habit of joking in conversation in order to hide this inner state of mine from the people around me.

After a pretty long time, when I grew calmer and realized after a rapid meditation that for the fulfillment of the object of my present journey to America, which among other things was connected with the financial question, it would be possible for me to manage without making use of this group of people, I decided while I was there, and after elucidating by personal contact with the people composing this group all the details and the shape of the gradual formation within their individuality of this original psychic peculiarity, I would do everything possible in order to uproot, if not from all, at least from the majority of them, this evil occasioned by the misunderstanding of my ideas, as well as some other causes, the nature of which I already half-guessed.

I must frankly confess that if such a strong reaction occurred in me, thanks to which I decided this time by all means to understand and elucidate from all sides the causes of this psychic peculiarity, and if possible to take all the corresponding measures, it was principally because in regard to people just of this group, long before, owing to their good attitude toward me during the hard years that followed my misfortune, there had long before gradually formed in me "something" commanding me to consider myself, in certain respects, under an obligation toward all of them in totality.

Well then, as the description of the events following this decision of mine may elucidate to every reader, among those who have become followers of my ideas, the causes of the arising of this fact maleficent in the objective sense and, for me personally, painfully distressing, and in order that perhaps some of them who have assimilated wrongly the essence of my ideas and who continue to apply them to themselves, so to say for their "welfare," I refer to those in whom data for common sense reflection are not yet completely atrophied-data which are formed in the psyche of man during his preparatory age may perhaps cease their so to say "self-ruination"; and furthermore, as acquaintance with the contents of the mentioned five talks delivered by me amidst people belonging to this very group during my two stays in New York which, by the way, were included among the measures I took for the rectification of these pernicious results "arisen through a misunderstanding of my ideas" may be, in my opinion, generally for every reader the "first flash of truth," I find it most fitting, as I have already said, to take the description of these events as a ground for the theme of this first book of the "edifying series" of my writings.

On the first evening of my arrival in New York, the 13th of November, 1930, there was arranged on the initiative of certain members of this group it must be presumed of "pure-blooded" Americans, judging by their ability to find ways of economizing time, a general meeting to enable them all to meet and personally greet me, in one of the studios of the famous theater, Carnegie Hall, to which I was invited by Mr. S. on the steamer as soon as it arrived in New York.

Mr. S. was at that time the official substitute for Mr. Orage who, thanks to certain conditions of ordinary life which were due principally to the misfortune which had occurred to me, became the first and chief representative of my ideas in America and also the principal guide of this particular group of Americans, and who was temporarily absent in England.

Most of those who had gathered there that evening were as it turned out personally known to me, that is to say, I had already met them either during my previous journeys to America or during their travels to France when they visited the Chateau du Prieure, which in recent years had been my permanent residence.

I went to this specially convened general meeting accompanied by several of my "translator-secretaries" *who* had arrived with me. During the first greetings and the famous "manipulation" called "shaking hands" I noticed in their faces and glances the same "something" that I had noticed among the people from Germany, England, Turkey, and other European countries who had also somehow or other become followers of my ideas. Then arose in me the data already mentioned, which had even before then been forming about these Americans and which after a little while brought me inwardly to the categorical decision, if it were not yet too late, to take certain corresponding measures for their welfare.

At the end of the "handshaking" and the interchange of all the usual vacuous words called "amiabilities" particularly used among Americans, I requested my secretary to read aloud the final chapter of the first series of my writings, which I had recently finished and which he had with him owing to the established custom of always having in his briefcase all my current work. I did this chiefly for the purpose of creating thus the necessary conditions for an unhindered observation of those present.

As to myself, sitting to one side in a corner, I began to observe attentively each of those present, and at the same time drew up in my thoughts a plan for further subsequent action in regard to all of them, as well as to each separately.

On that first evening, as it was late, I interrupted the reader in the middle of the chapter he was reading, and, addressing all present, promised first of all to arrange a general reading within the next few days in order to finish that chapter and went on to propose that they should choose three or four persons from among those present that evening, asking them to come to me in three days together with Mr. S., to decide collectively all the questions connected with my stay in New York.

True to say, I made this invitation with the premeditated purpose, in intimate talk with these four or five persons of sounding them out, of course indirectly, about various details which were not yet clear to me in connection with the suspicions which had arisen in me that evening during the reading, suspicions in this case related only to these American "sorry followers" of my ideas.

Expecting with indubitable certainty that this series of my expositions, as I have already said, will be really "edifyingly instructive," that is to say, will serve if only for the automatic formation in those creatures of Our Common Father, similar to myself, of data of all kinds, which ought to be, according to my understanding, present in a real man and not only of such data which are generally formed in the common presence of people, especially the contemporary ones, making them quite will-less, manifesting themselves in every way like mere animals, exclusively through the reflexes of the functioning of their organism, I want, right from the beginning of this series, to speak also of such external facts, the description of which for a naive reader might appear at first sight almost a meaningless, mere succession of words; whereas for a man who has the habit of thinking and of searching for the sense contained in so-called "allegorical expositions," on condition of a little strengthened mentation, they would be full of inner significance, and, if he makes the slightest effort "not to be a puppet of his automatic reflection," he will grasp and learn very much.

As perfect "showing material" for searching and understanding the inner sense in the description of similar, at first sight seemingly meaningless, external facts, there may serve what I said then at the end of the evening, on leaving the studio where this meeting had been arranged with the Americans gathered there to wish me personally welcome.

Walking out and pausing on the threshold, I turned round and addressing myself to them in that half-joking, half-serious tone at times proper to me, I said:

"Half-and-quarter powerful Gentlemen and to the extreme degree powerful Ladies of this 'dollar harvest continent' . . . I was very, very glad to see you and, although sitting so long among you this evening in the blissful sphere of your 'canned' radiations, there did develop energy enough perhaps even more than necessary for actualizing my aim for which I have this time come here to you; yet at the same time to the great misfortune I do not know, though, whether yours or mine there was imperceptibly again awakened in me that impulse I have always had, but which never acted during the time of my writing activity, namely, the impulse of pity for certain people who have reached majority, and whose vanitous parents or tutors, profiting from the absence in these future 'derelicts,' in their preparatory age, of their own wisdom, persuaded them, helping them with money, of course in a manner foreseen in Italian 'bookkeeping,' to become in their responsible age 'physician-psychiatrists,' in the present case for full-aged unfortunate people vegetating in American-scale organized 'lunatic asylums.'

"To speak frankly, I am not yet convinced of the exact cause of the reawakening in me of this previously existing undesirable impulse; as yet I only know that the reaction to these data began gradually to manifest itself owing to the fact that during the reading of the last chapter of the first series of my writings, while sitting in the corner and observing out of boredom the expressions on your faces, it seemed clear to me that there stood out on the forehead now of one, now of another of you, the inscription 'candidate for the madhouse.'

"I said 'out of boredom' because the contents of this chapter, over each sentence of which I had to think and again to think for three months almost day and night, bored me more than your fish called 'mackerel' which, during my first stay here, I was compelled to eat for six months morning and evening, it being the only fresh food you have."

After this, giving to my voice the tone which is taught in monasteries and is called "the tone of confused humbleness," I added:

"I am not yet certain if it really is so, or if it only seems so to me, as happens often in the psyche of a man who has experienced a great many 'troubles.' Owing to the six days of incessant pitching and rolling on the waves of the boundless ocean, and to the frequent introduction into myself of the noble French Armagnac and the constant regulating of its vibrations by the introduction into myself of the no less noble German 'hors d'oeuvres,' something in me is today, as it is said, 'fishy.' "

Three days after the significant American meeting just described days which the inhabitants there would characterize differently those having many dollars in their pockets, no matter what the ways of were obtaining them, as "passed with no monotony," while those for whom the absence of these dollars is chronic would say "the shortening by one more day of the approach of our last breath" the five aforementioned Americans came to me, headed by Mr. S.

Conversing with them about all kinds of naturally flowing associations and at the same time elucidating all the details I required concerning the suspicions that had arisen in me during the reading on the first evening of my arrival, I began to depict to them in relief all the already described constatations of mine in regard to the arising in the psyche of people, followers of my ideas, of this strange peculiarity and the perspectives ensuing from this and then, speaking briefly about the reasons for my present coming to America and the impossibility for me to spare much of my time for the members of their group, I requested them to avoid what had happened during these days when, on account of visits of one or another member of the group and their sometimes quite idiotic questions, I had not the opportunity to write a single word.

I therefore proposed to them to form a kind of committee and to take upon themselves the work of organizing twice a week general meeting of the members of their group, at which I would always try to be present and also, to see to it that on other days nobody should disturb me by personal visits, by letters or even by telephone.

After this, we decided together, in order to economize my time and also for many other considerations, to hold the proposed general meeting in my apartment and, in view of the limited size of the largest room there, which was a kind of hall, not to admit to these meetings more than fifty persons and, for the remaining members of the group, to arrange meetings in the studios of Carnegie Hall or in other private rooms where, without my necessarily being present, there should be read aloud by one of my translator-secretaries everything taken down in shorthand of the questions that had been asked me, and my answers to them.

As a conclusion, I begged them as yet not to tell anything of what I had said that day to any of the members of their group and added:

"According to the deductions after the observations and questionings made by me during these days, to my great regret, I shall be compelled during my present stay in New York to take various measures toward many of your comrades in order that either they should become completely disappointed in my ideas or there should disappear the faith crystallized in their individuality during these years in regard to Mr. Orage and his authority."

FIRST TALK

delivered by me on November 28th, 1930, with free entrance into the assemblage of everyone without exception of the followers of my ideas belonging to the mentioned group

I began thus:

Today and the day before, I seriously meditated upon how I should find such a method for my explanations, by the totality of which I intend today, and in the two or three following meetings, to make clear for you certain definite information having a close connection with your life, and to give a shape and sequence to my expositions, such as might perhaps, in the conditions created by you North Americans in the sense of abnormally great as compared with other people's mechanism of mentation contribute to a normal and impartial comprehension by you of this definite information.

I had to ponder over it long and seriously chiefly because of my sincere desire, now that I have the possibility, to give you some help by my explanations, you Americans composing just this group of the followers of my ideas, as people toward whom, during the period of my intercourse with you, thanks to your kind attitude toward me personally and to my work in the hard years after the misfortune which happened to me, there was formed and still is present now constantly functioning so to say "life-giving data" for benevolence; besides, in the same period a firm conviction gradually formed itself in me that in all of you, obviously thanks to an abnormally superfluous reading of newspaper literature, there developed, more than in other people, that abnormal psychic factor which in the last centuries has generally become an imprescriptible inherency of contemporary people and which very definitely, as it can be easily proved experimentally, acts on the general psyche of people in such a way as to contribute to their being satisfied by superficial assimilation of all kinds of new impressions read or heard, without evoking in them the forebodings of any bad consequences from this.

As a result of these reflections, I think I succeeded finally in working out in my thoughts an approximately corresponding form of exposition.

In accordance with this so to say "scheme of exposition," I shall now first of all arouse in you and explain several such questions which, as I presume, will appear on first sight quite unfitting for what you expect to hear from me in the sense of what I have promised to say with respect to your welfare, whereas in reality only such a scheme of sequential development of the promised explanations may, in my opinion, crystallize in your abnormally constructed "mental apparatus" those notions, the cognition of which I consider not only very useful for you but absolutely indispensable.

First of all, I want to acquaint you with two of the fundamental points of that detailed program worked out by me which was predetermined for gradual introduction into the life of people by means of the Institute for the Harmonious Development of Man founded by me.

This Institute, by the way, was first founded by me while still in Russia, two years before the beginning of, as one calls it now, "the World War," but I could not succeed in establishing firmly this "child" of mine, as one says, "on its own legs" in spite of many repeated attempts to set it up in various other countries which ended every time, thanks to all kinds of consequences of this war, with a "crash," accompanied for me with enormous material loss and waste of effort, which demanded almost superhuman tension of my physical and moral strength until, as I have already said, eight years ago, in noble France.

One of the paragraphs of the mentioned circumstantial program included a detailed working out for the actualization of that plan of mine, namely, that as soon as the economic question was more or less established in the main section of the Institute and in the other sections already organized at about that time, and there was also more or less established the process of assimilation of a so-called "comprehension" in the nature of people working upon themselves who lived in the mentioned sections, I would begin at once to organize with the help of people who had already reached in these sections a definite degree, as it was called in all previously existing esoteric schools, of "being and comprehension," in every big city of the continents of Asia, Europe and North America in which are concentrated the interests of big agglomerations of people of the given special group, public institutions of a new type, similar to the "clubs" existing at the present day almost everywhere in the ordinary life of people, and to introduce into the internal life of such public institutions of a new type instead of what is already established in such particular places for a definite group of people, that is, their own regulations, principles, religious and economic opinions, etc., and instead of the already established pastimes, that is to say, reading newspapers and periodicals, playing cards, arranging balls and masquerades and various concerts, which generally, especially in these days, proceed with the "gentle participation" of those who in the opinion of the majority of con-temporary people are "known" and "famous" and, in my opinion, with the participation principally of such people who, on account of the abnormal life of their ancestors as well as their own, represent nothing more than the types who in the period of Babylonian civilization were designated as "moving sources of an evil radiation", well then, instead of all that, usually proceeding in similar clubs, which gives absolutely nothing for the welfare of their members and the real development of their individuality, to introduce the habit of getting acquainted gradually and in strict sequence, through common reading, lectures and explanations given by people specially prepared for this purpose and sent from the mentioned sections, with various fragments of that totality of theoretical information, on the principles of which the Institute founded by me is based, namely, that totality of information, accessible to the comprehension of each contemporary man, after learning which, everybody must acknowledge that, even if all this is not yet known in the life of people, it is at the same time by its truth as axiomatic as for instance that "when it rains, the pavements are wet," so that this may become, of everything that one is required to cognize in order to lead a life suitable for man and not for a wild animal, really the most important, even more indispensable than the air we breathe, and then afterwards, on the basis of and in accordance with the conviction obtained thanks to such theoretical information regarding the possibility and also the very means of achievement of the required data for one's own welfare, to undertake together the actualization of all this in practice.

The second of these points, in my opinion indispensable for you to know, included the detailed working out and form of actualization of that supposition of mine, in order, with the establishment of a more or less balanced "tempo" of life in the main section of the Institute, to subdivide immediately all the pupils, according to the results obtained in their subjective inner work upon themselves, into three independent groups named: the first exoteric, outer group; the second mesoteric, middle group; and the third esoteric, inner group.

To the first, exoteric group were to belong all those who had newly entered, as well as those who had not yet acquired by their subjective merits the right to belong to the second, the mesoteric group.

The pupils belonging to this second, mesoteric group, according to the fundamental program, were to be as yet initiated only theoretically into all the questions not accessible to the average man which have been elucidated by me personally owing to my half a century's special searching's both on my own and together with a specially organized group of people of the highest contemporary culture, who devoted themselves to the search for objective truth.

The members of the third group, the esoteric, according to the same detailed program, were to be initiated not only theoretically into all these questions, but also practically, and to be introduced to all the means for a real possibility of self-perfecting, but of course only after having been for a long time experimentally tried and verified in quite exceptionally planned circumstances.

With the members of this third group, it is opportune to say, I just intended to devote myself to the searching for means already accessible to everyone and to the applying of all that was learned thus and minutely verified for the welfare of all humanity.

Now I want still, chiefly for the purpose of forming in your, as I have already said, "never on earth so completely mechanized mentation," an approximate, as the ancient learned psychologists called it, "linking ground for logical confrontation" of my future explanations, as well as in order that you could already, though approximately, as it is said, "guess" why I mentioned just these two points and what relation they may have for my future projected explanations concerning your welfare, and I even find indispensable, in accordance with the same scheme of sequential explanations, previously composed in my thoughts, before speaking of what has an immediate relation to you, to tell, or better to confess that, among several very definite so-called "initiative factors," gradually crystallized in my "subjectivism," thanks to intensive, not very agreeable experiencing's repeated many times during the period of the working out and applying in life of the mentioned program, there are two such factors which always, when acting as a result of lawful causes, almost every time provoke in the mental and feeling associations and experiencing a feeling, not assimilated without difficulty, of "bitterness."

The first of these "initiative psychic factors," which even till the present time often enervates me, formed itself in me just at the time of working out this program thanks to an unremitting fight between themselves of my consciousness and my nature.

I must tell you that, many years ago, before the organization of the Institute, when I planned and worked out this program in detail, not only did I have to address myself for advice and direction concerning several questions to honorable and impartial people from among those I eventually had the happiness to meet in the course of my life, and who, by the way, contrary to the opinion existing in people on the lawfulness of the established limit of human life, had already overcome two centuries of their existence and some of whom were bold enough to hope to surmount even the third century, but also, concerning several special questions, I had often to consult various in no way remarkable people who, although they belonged to the number of authorities on certain notions in contemporary life, concerning these questions were at the same time, as is usual for this kind of contemporary people, thoroughly "stuffed" with all kinds of such "beautiful properties" as "conceit," "vanity," "ambition," "flattery" and so on.

The fact that at that time I had with very great inner effort, as one says, "to experience" and in my external relations to reckon with it, constituted the primary data for the formation in me of the first of the mentioned "initiative factors."

The second of the mentioned "psychic factors" formed itself already there on the continent of Europe in the second year after I finally settled down in France in conditions, as I have already said, more or less favorable and began to work in accordance with the previously mentioned worked-out program; and the formation of this factor was due to the results of the "self-content" of several people who were in contact with me in the following conditions of my activity at that time.

Notwithstanding the inevitable necessity from the very first day of my arrival in Europe to consecrate not less than half of my physical and psychic forces for the regulation of the great financial crisis created some time before, on account of the "ignominious stupidity" of the Russian power-possessing people, and notwithstanding that I had to consecrate the other half of the time to the theoretical explanation and practical teaching of the seventy pupils who were being specially prepared for the demonstrations of so to say illustrative material that were supposed to be held everywhere in Europe and America the next year, with the aim of showing the results of the application in life of my new ideas, nevertheless I succeeded in directing my work so that, already by the beginning of the second year of the existence of the Institute in France, data were formed in me as well as in all the people who had a contact with me, and who were more or less in the current of my instructions, for a strong conviction that very soon it would be possible to realize also in practice both of the points just explained by me in the mentioned detailed program, that is to say: to classify all the pupils living in the Institute into three separate groups, and to begin with each group the previously foreseen "theoretical" and "practical" studies and, at the same time, to organize in the places where the interests of big agglomerations of people are concentrated the mentioned "clubs" of a new type.

Unfortunately, nothing of the concrete consequences for general human welfare expected from this program, which had been foreseen in the smallest details, could be realized, on account of the event known to all of you which happened to me six years ago and which many learned and ordinary people and all those who knew me and who heard about it attributed with their usual superficial understanding merely to a "motor accident," although in reality as I supposed from the first when I recovered my senses, and as I am now quite convinced, it was the last chord of the manifestation toward me of that "something" usually accumulating in the common life of people, which, as is mentioned by me in *The Herald of Coming Good,* was first noticed by the Great, really Great King of Judea, Solomon, and was called "Tzvarnoharno."

Returning to a more detailed description of the facts of that time, which is necessary for your understanding of my present explanations, one must say that from the very beginning, when everything was more or less established for the ordinary existence of a great number of people in the two houses purchased by me in France called the Chateau du Prieure and Le Paradou, and the construction of a special large building which afterwards was known to you under the name of the "Study House" had been finished in haste, I began an almost daily series of lectures for the pupils of the Institute, those who had newly entered there in Europe as well as those who had come with me from Russia and those who had joined during my wanderings from the Caucasus to Europe when, owing to all kinds of political complications, it had been impossible to actualize even a single paragraph of the mentioned program or to settle anywhere permanently, to elucidate parallel with the previous, superficial outline, the details which in their totality illustrated the essence of my ideas, and to explain more substantially only that part from among twenty-four subdivisions of the general totality of the exposition of my ideas, the assimilation of which is absolutely obligatory for anyone to begin a productive work upon himself.

For your better understanding of the further explanations given by me then, I consider it indispensable to repeat some of them now.

Among other things, I said then that the most important work for a man who has already cognized with his Reason his real significance that is to say, who has cognized his error in the sense of the exaggerated importance given to his individuality, which represents, according to his own impartial appreciation in a quiet state, almost a complete "nullity" is to acquire the ableness to direct for a definite time all his possibilities and all his strength only for the purpose of constating as many as possible of the physical as well as the psychic abnormal facts proceeding in his various functioning's, that is, to exercise what is called "self-observation."

It is obligatorily necessary to do so chiefly in order that such undesirable facts, cognized only by his mind, which are still empty of significance for his common presence, gradually assimilating into his nature, should begin to crystallize a steady conviction about everything learned, and through this, as it must lawfully proceed, should come forth in his common presence for the possibility of further work upon himself, an energy of great intensiveness, with the help of which alone is a further work upon himself possible and which is manifested, by the way, in a persistent striving to achieve the "power" during the daytime in his so to say "waking state," for a definite time, to "remember himself."

This is necessary in its turn so that such a man, who has cognized only in his mind the nullity of his individuality and who has decided to struggle consciously with the abnormalities constated by him, which have crystallized in his individuality thanks to the unfitting surrounding conditions of his preparatory age, and which manifest themselves in all sorts of weaknesses that in totality give birth to his will-lessness, character-lessness, inertness and so on, could learn as much as possible not to identify with the surrounding conditions and, continuing to observe his inner and outer manifestations with a simultaneous domination in himself of various feelings of partiality which are becoming inherent in him, and thus constating still more deeply various factors, abnormal even according to his own consciousness, and existing in great number in his psyche as well as in his physical body: all this *with* the aim of convincing himself with his whole being of his negative properties that are even in his own judgment unworthy of a man, and not only with his, in the present case, meaning-nothing "mind"; so that thus he may again become a person wishing to work upon himself with his whole being, and not only, as I have just said, with his meaningless consciousness.

On account of the great importance of this question, I repeat and underline that all this is indispensable in order that in a man working upon himself should arise and accumulate, as could only lawfully proceed, the needed energy for the possibility of continuing to work with the intensity of striving and power of action upon himself which alone permits the transmutation of oneself from this "nullity" into that "something," which he ought to have been according to even his own "good sense"; this latter, although rarely, does manifest itself in each contemporary man at those moments when the surrounding conditions do not prevent the manifestation of this good sense, that is, to be such as a man ought to be, the, as is said, "acme of Creation," and not what he has become in reality, especially in recent times, namely, as in moments of self-sincerity he knows himself to be an automatically perceiving and in everything manifesting himself domestic animal.

Now I shall speak to you in the form of a conspectus about the events which provoked the causes of my first journey to you in America.

When, in the heat of my already described activity, repeated troubles began to grow again on a great scale in that "fertile soil for the growth of all kinds of scandals" bearing the name Russia, troubles which were related to me personally only because there were living with me many of those unfortunate biped creatures, toward whom by the Will of Fate there had been formed in me "something" constantly reminding and obliging me to contribute to the possible continuation of the breathing of such inevitably existing cosmic arisings, whom Great Nature, considering the complexity of the apparatus for an easy assimilation of air by the organism, and obviously on account of lack of time, had deprived of this apparatus, with the result that my poor "Minister of Finance" could not restrain himself and again and again cried out "Help, help!", I was compelled to make the decision, without waiting for the complete preparation of the material I had planned upon, to travel immediately to you Americans people covered at that time with so to say "a dollar deposit" with only that material which had been already more or less prepared.

On my first arrival at that time in America and during the six months' stay here among you, I had not only successfully enough regulated the "material question" of the Institute, but also prepared everything required for the foundation here in

America of several permanent sections.

Having fully convinced myself then of the possibility in the future in North America of realizing broad plans connected with my ideas, I at once without losing time opened here in New York, by the way, temporary classes in rhythmic movements and in music with the intention on my next visit, which was supposed to be six months later, of transforming these classes into the first fundamental branch of the Institute in America.

Just in that phase of my activity for the introduction into life for the welfare of people of the program which had been worked out in all details, there occurred, almost immediately after my return to Europe, that "misfortune" which, besides preventing among other things my intended journey here, became, so to say, the germ of all the subsequent misunder-standings which had an equal relation to my ideas and also of course to me personally.

The beginning of the multiplication and nourishing of these misunderstandings, already previously existing in great number in relation to me and to the process for the actualization of my intentions, as well as the scattering of new ones as if from a horn of plenty, was due chiefly to the fact that for several months after this "misfortune" I lost my memory entirely and then for several months more lay in a semiconscious state.

The soil for a plentiful flourishing of all kinds of misunderstandings connected with my ideas became extraordinarily fecund because after the mentioned misfortune, when I began gradually to recover my usual powers of combination and memory and, thanks to the reasons already described by me in the last chapter of the first series of my writings, began to liquidate the main section as well as all the other sections of the Institute founded by me, which was established on a new basis according to the Statute of the Institute, people living there of every degree of "being and comprehension," most of whom belonged to various independent nations composing the population of the old Russian Empire, having no possibility of returning to their motherland, as in all these places there continued that psychosis of the masses which began some years previously, were obliged, on account of unexpected circumstances, to disperse to various countries in Europe, and to England and even America, depending on where they had friends or relatives, and most of these previous pupils of my Institute, when they found themselves dispersed and had fallen into hard conditions, as still continues to be the case for almost all the "refugees" from this previously rich Russia, having no data necessary for a normal earning of life in the local conditions, probably suddenly remembered crumbs of the general quantity of information they had heard at the Institute and profiting, consciously or unconsciously that has no importance for the given case from the general unbalanced-ness of mind arisen as a lawful consequence of the World War, decided to "prophesize" my new ideas.

As each of these pupils of the Institute founded by me, in the sense of his "subjective being," belonged as yet only to the mentioned exoteric group, that is to say, still had the being of an ordinary average man and consequently possessed fully the inherencies which are proper to contemporary man, among which, obligatorily and inevitably, is this, that he can be interested and take in from everything new to him only what corresponds to his own already-established subjectivity and make it the center of gravity of his mentation, they, taking this as a basis, began among the people-victims of the mentioned "unbalanced-ness of mind" to prophesize in a one sided way verbally, as well as by literature, the information assimilated by them "one bit here and one bit there" which they had heard from me personally or from my old pupils who were prepared by me for a future spreading of my ideas on a large scale.

Here it is interesting to note that at that time my own self almost ceased so to say "to annoy" the attention of these people who were more or less acquainted with my instructions.

From the numerous definite facts elucidated during my recent special observations in regard to the causes of the arising of a certain specific property in the psyche of people who have become followers of my ideas, I think that it will be, for now, enough to note, by the way, that at present, for all the people existing in different countries who have in one way or another become followers of my ideas, the totality of data for their psychic functioning, which in general crystallizes in people thanks to various surrounding mechanical influences, becomes afterwards an automatically stimulating factor for the manifestation of their subjectivity, as a result of which these people during their automatically flowing associations, as well as in the times of their half-conscious exchange of opinions among themselves, are animated by the necessity of arguing with enthusiasm and persistency, creating thus a really perceived and very intensively manifested idee fixe, relating only to certain, sometimes quite insignificant information, which clears up only one particular question from the numberless questions which exclusively by their whole totality compose and elucidate the essence of my ideas.

For instance, in the so to say "consciousness" of people existing in one part of Russia, from the general totality of information which had been given to them and which they took in certainly "a bit here and a bit there," only that part was firmly crystallized which among other things explains theoretically by analogous examples the fact that the common presence of man is composed of three independently formed and educated parts, and on that alone they base the probable truth of all my ideas; in a number of people existing in another part of Russia, thanks to some fragments of the explained and proved information, there was crystallized in their consciousness the one idea that a man who has never worked intentionally on his perfecting is deprived not only of a soul but also of spirit.

People from Germany, especially those from Bavaria, thanks to the information assimilated by them about the possibility of an effective nutrition not only with the ordinary food but also with air, have taken as their "fancy" the idea of giving to the composition of their blood the property of being able to fulfill all the exigencies of the physical body and at the same time to contribute to the crystallization and perfecting of the astral body.

People from the capital of England were so to say "crazy" about, or better say "it suited their English soul" and became the *idee fixe* of their psyche, that summing-up conclusion of the general totality of my theoretical information, which is formulated by the expression "to remember oneself and which was indicated as a necessity.

People living in contemporary northern Greece preferred, and made the center of gravity of their interest in my ideas, the so to say, "law of seven" and the "three existing aspects" of every event, and so on.

As for you Americans, composing just this group, your *idée fixe* is based on separate fragments, taken in by you also "one bit here and one bit there," of that unique general part from the twenty-four sections already mentioned by me forming the fundamental fractions of the general totality of information explaining theoretically all my ideas, about which I said lately that this part concerns the question of "self-observation" and underlined that this information is inevitably required at the beginning of work upon oneself.

SECOND TALK

*delivered by me in the same place to
a much-increased assemblage*

Last time, in the second half of my talk, I spoke about the supposition crystallized in me regarding the probable causes of the arising, as a result of wrongly interpreted ideas of mine, of a very undesirable particularity in the general psyche of people from various independent groups; today, I shall begin my explanations about the same, but exclusively in regard to you Americans previously composing as well as presently belonging to this group of people who have also become followers of my ideas.

Now, I want to present on this subject, after my special observations and investigations during these last days, an already completely determined opinion regarding just how and in what sequence were formed also among you here the conditions for the crystallization in your psyche of that pernicious factor on account of which, now, in most of you, to my sincere regret, instead of finding, in comparison with other people, data of a "higher level" which obligatorily ought to have been formed during this time in you, as people who happened prematurely to come in contact with the truths learned by me through my half-century's conscientious labors, almost incomprehensible for contemporary people, which give the possibility and chance to every man to obtain the Being of a real man there is formed, as I can now impartially constate, something quite contrary.

Frankly speaking, almost every one of you gives the impression of, and really is, a man who has all the data to become at any moment a client of one of those, on an American scale, organized houses in New York which are called "madhouses", and which are supported here by the followers of the English suffragettes.

For you Americans, the arising of this evil which formed itself in connection with my ideas began and gradually took a definite form thanks to the following events:

When, as I have already said, at the beginning of the second year of the existence of the Institute in France, I was compelled to take the decision, without waiting for the complete preparation of the material for demonstrations, to travel immediately to you Americans in order that here, among you, types still foreign to me, I should not be compelled to "live on beans mixed with thumbtacks" with such a large number of people indispensable for the realization of the aims I had in view, each of whom to my misfortune as well as, later on, to the misfortune of many of your compatriots who have become through them the objects of my periodic chief specialty, which is "to shear half the wool of every near comer" was at that period subject to a disease which in the psyche of the patient evokes, among other things, the habit of having in his pockets exclusively "a louse on a leash" in one and in the other "a flea on a chain," I considered it a necessary preliminary then, in order that at least something might be prepared here in New York for the arrival of such great numbers of people, to send there, on the last boat sailing just before ours, someone from among my trusted and experienced people.

In consequence of the fact that, just a short time before this, most of my "pupils of the first rank," as they called themselves, who were suitable for this purpose, had been sent by me for aims in the common interest to various European and Asiatic countries on special missions, my choice, from among those who were near me, of the most suitable person for this preliminary departure fell upon one of the older followers of my ideas, who was then the chief physician of the Institute, Dr. Stjernvall, but as, at that time, he was not at all acquainted with the English language, I decided to send together with him, as assistant and translator, one of the newly entered English pupils.

Examining in my mind and considering the usefulness of each one separately for such a journey, I decided to send just this English pupil, from the number of those newly entered in the Institute, who, according to the so-called "individual record" usually made in the Institute for each pupil, was previously an English journalist and, I thought, as a journalist ought surely to know English very well.

This former English journalist predetermined by me at first to be a translator and assistant of the first person sent by me to America as so to say "messenger of my new ideas," Dr. Stjernvall, and who a little later became the collaborator of my personal translator, M. Ferapontov, a pupil of the Institute and a participant in the demonstrations of "rhythmic movements," who toward the end of my stay here became one of the three as they were then called "managers," that is to say, organizers of demonstrations, lectures and business interviews with different people I had to see was nobody else than that man who, on account of fortuitous circumstances, arising partly from the catastrophe which happened to me and partly from the consequences of that abnormality at the basis of family life, crystallized in the life of contemporary people, especially in you Americans, which consists in the fact that the leading role in the household belongs to the woman, afterwards became your chief leader; I speak, as you yourself surely have already guessed, of Mister Orage.

All the following, which led to the sad results that are the object of our talk of today, arose in the following successiveness:

When, at the end of my first visit to America, after a rather successful realization of all my plans, I was ready to go back to Europe with the intention, as I said then, to return in six months for the purpose of already opening permanent branches of the Institute in some of your big cities, and, several days before my departure, I was discussing aloud, together with the people who came with me, who could be left here for the continuation of what had been begun as well as various other preparations for my next intended arrival, Mr. Orage, being present as well, unexpectedly offered his services and with great excitement began to affirm his able-ness to do it brilliantly.

As I found him quite suitable for the necessary preparations, chiefly on account of his proven knowledge of the English language, of which I had been convinced already here in New York, as well as on account of his smart appearance which, as might be easily understood, has a great importance in all business relations, especially among you Americans, I accepted his offer and began to explain to him at once certain details of the required preparations.

As I learned afterwards, the real cause of his offer and his enthusiasm was that during our stay in New York he had started a romance, which at this time was at its apogee, with a saleswoman of that bookshop with the very original name "Sunwise Turn," where I began there in New York among a very small number of your compatriots, according to my habit, to hold meetings in the form of lecture talks, answering among other things different questions which were asked me regarding my ideas.

Well then, as I have already said, on my return to Europe after my sojourn among you, at the end of the first week there occurred to me that motor accident, as a result of which for over three months I entirely lost my memory and powers of combination, and then for six months more lay in a semiconscious state, half controlling these two fundamental capacities on which depend and which generally impose responsibility on the individuality of man, and when as a consequence of all this a great crisis arose in all my affairs gradually taking proportions which announced a complete catastrophe, then I, just at the beginning of this said second period of my physical state, still quite helpless in body and kept in bed, clearly realizing in lucid intervals of my consciousness the created situation, began, on the one hand, to give orders and take all kinds of measures for the most rapid liquidation of everything connected with the Institute on account of the constantly required great expense with a complete lack of revenues, and also the absence among the people round me of a "businessman," and, on the other hand, to invent all kinds of combinations for the regulation of innumerable misunderstandings, arising thanks to the mentioned liquidation as well as to the pernicious manifestations of various types usually proceeding, as I have said, among degenerated people of our class.

Then, by the way, once, just in that period when the functioning of my usual powers of combination began to be reestablished from time to time, and I could realize clearly what had happened and imagine different possibilities as a way out of the situation that had been created, one of the people near me, who at that time acted as my financial minister, addressing himself to me about one financial embarrassment, the solving of which was above his capacities, said to me that just that day he had received from America, from Mr. Orage, $1, 000, adding that it was the third time that he had received such a sum and that it always came most appropriately.

In the following months, as my state was still almost without change and during the mentioned lucid periods, I could hardly discuss the affairs regarding the liquidation or find diverse combinations for the purpose of getting out of the desperate situation which had been created, I entirely forgot about Mr. Orage and his kind solicitude in regard to me and my work.

Only a year after the mentioned talk about money sent by Mr. Orage from America, when I had more or less liquidated all the dangers of the advancing catastrophe and the state of my health had improved, I found out that these "sendings" from Mr. Orage, though diminished, still continued, and that some of your compatriots participated in them. Just then, I at once changed my mind regarding my first decision to shut the doors of my house to all people, making an exception for you Americans composing just this group as well as for all Americans who showed an interest in my ideas, and, from then on, not only were the doors of my house always open for you but with some of you, about whose real interest in my ideas I was informed beforehand by somebody who had already proved his faithfulness in the sense of real interest in my new ideas, I, as much as my deep occupation with serious questions of my writings would permit, was always willing to have talking relations also.

As regards the immediate cause for the formation in your mentation of the mentioned *idee fixe*, which served in its turn as a factor for the gradual crystallization in your psyche of the mentioned specific particularity, all that, as I represent it to myself now, after detailed confrontations and so to say "statistical deductions" based on personal inquiries of several members of this very group as well as others near to them, probably happened in the following way:

Mr. Orage, who was left by me in America and who was occupied at first only by fulfilling my errands regarding my projected second visit, after the catastrophe which occurred to me, while very much captivated by my ideas, and still not yet completely under the influence of his "left-shoulder Angel," when he learned of all that had occurred to me, at once began profiting from the strong impression still continuing by inertia which I had made on your compatriots, and for several months began to collect money and to send a part of it to me at the Prieure.

And at the same time, obviously with the aim of giving an external justification to these collections, he began, without my permission for it, to direct the classes for "rhythmic movements" organized by me here in New York; furthermore, realizing the necessity and at the same time all the difficulties of getting means on the one hand for sending money to me, and on the other hand for meeting the excessive expenditures of his new family life as by this time his romance had ended in his marrying the saleswoman of "Sunwise Turn," a young American pampered out of all proportion to her position he began, for the purpose of increasing his resources, to organize, as was usual in the Institute life, talks on themes which he had learned during his stay in the Institute.

When all this material had been used up by him, not receiving either any new material or any definite indication from me as to what to do or how to proceed further, he had willy-nilly to get along during this time merely with what he had assimilated during his stay in the Institute while still in the capacity of an ordinary pupil and, with this very limited knowledge, to so to say "manipulate in every way."

As I only recently elucidated to myself during my present

sojourn here by inquiring of some of your comrades who were members, from the beginning, of the group which Mr. Orage directed, he, like a good "juggler," managed with only the primary information, out of the whole totality of information throwing light on all my ideas, which concerned that question about which I spoke in the last lecture, that is to say, the question of so-called "self-observation," namely, with the summarized elucidation of this information, the knowledge of which is indeed quite indispensable at the beginning for everyone who is striving to learn the truth, but which, if it becomes the center of gravity for the mentation of man, will, as was long ago established and verified by me, unfailingly lead to just the result which, to my great regret, I observe now in almost every one of you.

This situation, created at the beginning of my writing activity on account of the catastrophe which occurred to me, continued until the present time.

Now, after an interruption of seven years in the application in life by successive stages of the mentioned detailed program which had become the aim and sense of my life, having finally finished this principal and most difficult task, which required constantly all my attention and all my self-imposed efforts during these years, I want, simultaneously with fulfilling the easier part of my task, to renew the actualization of this aim of mine but this time, with the help of the results obtained during these past years from my constant intensive labors realized in ten big volumes; namely, I intend to continue to give a final polishing to my writings, in order to make them accessible to the understanding of every average man and, while doing this work in the same conditions as before, that is to say, writing in various cafés, restaurants or other public places, always traveling, to begin simultaneously with this to make these accidental or intentional sojourns in different centers of contemporary civilization, which satisfy the required conditions, the preparation of the soil for the organization of the clubs mentioned by me last time.

As my present visit here coincides with the moment for creating conditions which will give me the possibility of undertaking the realization of my plans, I have therefore decided, during the period of my stay here among you, to devote all the time left after the fulfillment of my fundamental task to the organization and opening here of the first club of this kind.

The opening here in New York, with the participation of people composing this group of yours, of the first branch, not only in North America but in general on Earth, of the main club which will be in France at the Chateau du Prieure, will be in my opinion in all respects right and objectively just.

It will be right and just because the Americans, chiefly you who compose this group, besides having been for a long time in contact with my ideas, were the only ones who proved to be grateful to me during the hard years of crisis, and you were also the only ones with whom I had personal relations after the misfortune which occurred to me, when I gave my-self fully to my new profession as a writer and broke all relationships I had previously had with people of every rank and class in various European states of course excluding my relations with the employees of various cafes and restaurants.

Well then, my friends imposed by Destiny! In spite of my most natural sincere desire, which must be clear to you, that the first branch of the "fundamental kernel" of such a first institution connected with my ideas should be organized just here among you, I, impartially analyzing with my consciousness all the past and confronting certain obvious facts, cannot fulfill in peace such a wish, dear to my nature.

The cause of such a contradiction in my general inner state is my clear understanding of the fact that some of you, perhaps on account of always being such, or on account of various misunderstandings which took place in the past years in the internal life of your group, do not correspond at all to the requirements which must be put before the members of this first institution proposed to be organized here, namely, such an institution which in my opinion must have for the future a very important character of general human significance.

During the time of my presence here among you, more than once I seriously thought about the situation which had been created but failed to find a definite way out of it, and only today, when it appeared clear that I shall be obliged to come here again next year on account of some business which has no connection whatever with you, and I realized, besides, that I should be for at least one year or even more occupied with questions concerning my writings, I took a categorical decision: to postpone the organization of these clubs until next year and to devote all the time left of my present stay among you entirely to the personal reorganization of your group, in this sense, to introduce into its internal life principles corresponding to my ideas which must unfailingly be actualized and which could contribute, in the general psyche of some of you, to the accelerated crystallization of corresponding data for the possibility of being deemed worthy of becoming, by the time of my visit to you next year, competent "kernel-composing" members of the said first institution and principles which contribute, in the general psyche of others, data for a sincere confession of their unworthiness to be members of this first model institution with the result that they, having understood this, withdraw themselves. In other words, to consecrate all my free time, first, to establishing personally in the required tempo everything corresponding for a right work with the person whom I intend to send to you for directing everything that is necessary for that attainment in strict accordance with my ideas of my fixed aims and, second, to purifying your group of those elements, which in the existing conditions not only cannot gain any profit for themselves, but may, for the formation as well as the actualizing of the general aim in this newly formed group, be very, very pernicious.

The second part of this plan designed by me, that is to say, the purification of undesirable elements from your group, will manifest itself from the very beginning of the formation of this new group because there will be placed before its members among other things several very definite conditions, allowing of no compromise whatsoever, to which in all probability not all of you will be able to agree, and in this way some of the members of the former group will naturally fall away.

Thirteen such unfailingly required obligatory conditions for the right to be a member of this new group during the first months of its existence will be laid down by me; seven of these will be of "objective character," that is to say, will concern everyone and must be fulfilled by all without exception, and six will be of "subjective character," that is to say, will concern personally those of the former members of the old group, for whom personally these conditions will be made.

Concerning the subjective conditions, it must be said that their character will ensue from the elucidations I have already made or still intend to make either myself or through those whom I shall commission concerning the specific subjectivity of each of you, formed owing to a certain kind of psychic data arisen thanks to typicality, heredity and also acquired during the period of equal-rights membership in the former group.

Detailed explanation of the significance of all thirteen conditions, and the explanation of the motives logically justifying the necessity of these conditions, will be given by me in advance exclusively to those members of the former group who agree to and bind themselves under a special oath, the form of which I shall indicate partly at once, partly later on, to fulfill exactly the first of the aforementioned seven objective conditions.

Having said this, I called my secretary and dictated to him the following:

"I, undersigned, after mature and profound reflection, without being influenced by anyone else at all, but of my own free will, promise under oath not to have, without instructions from MR. GURDJIEFF or a person officially representing him, any relations whatsoever, spoken or written, with any of the members of the former group existing till now under the name of 'Orage's group' of the followers of MR. GURDJIEFF'S ideas and also not to have any relations without the special permission of MR. GURDJIEFF or his substitute with Mr. Orage himself.

"I am to have relations exclusively with those members of the former group, a list of whose names will be given to me during the general meetings of the newly formed exoteric group."

Having read aloud the text of this obligation, I said:

"Finishing today with this our meeting, I will merely add the following:

"Those of you who, as is said in the text of the paper I have just read, agree 'after mature and profound reflection' to sign this paper must do so before twelve o'clock noon the day after tomorrow in the presence of my secretary-translator.

"As to when and where the first general meeting of this new exoteric group will be held, all those who have signed the paper by the time set will be informed in due course."

———————

THIRD TALK

*delivered by me to a pretty rarefied
assemblage*

I began thus:

In order that all my explanations and elucidations, as well as the lectures and reports of different instructors specially prepared for applying my ideas practically in life, whom it is my intention from this year to adjoin to your group from time to time also, should be productive and give real results during your future general meetings and your private encounters and exchanges of opinion, in other words, in order that all your talks having relation to my ideas should not assume such a character as they have had till now, namely, as I have recently called them, "meetings for collective titillation," I want today, already at this what may be called "first meeting on new principles," to give you, as a sop to say precept, some advice which has relation only to you Americans in general and especially to those composing the given group, the infallible fulfilling of which advice may alone, in my opinion, in the now created conditions, stop the development of the disastrous consequences of the causes provoked by the errors in the past.

This benevolent advice of mine to you Americans, composing

in the given case this group, and who became, thanks to a series of accidentally arranged circumstances of life, my nearest essential friends, consists in indicating the categorical necessity that each of you should cease entirely, at least for three months, the reading of your newspapers and magazines, and during this time should become as well acquainted as possible with the contents of all three books of the first series of my writings entitled *An Objectively Impartial Criticism of the Life of Man.*

An acquaintance with the contents of these books is quite indispensable for each of you, chiefly in order to obtain directly or indirectly information elucidated from all sides regarding all those definite notions upon which will be based, and from which will logically derive all the problems which are pursued for practical attainments. It was just for this purpose that your group was organized and is now reorganized to consist of people who have more or less cognized the absurdity of our ordinary life and who, although you have not yet sensed it with all your Being but are seriously striving to take in what you have cognized, are continuing to learn as many aspects of the objective truth as possible so as to determine, in accordance with this, your own real individuality, in order to manifest afterwards in everything in a way corresponding to a Godlike creature.

It must be said that all I have expounded in the three books of the first series in its totality embraces almost all the questions which in my opinion, formed on the basis of long years of experimental elucidations, may arise under the conditions of contemporary life in the ordinary mentation of man, and the elucidation of all these questions has been made by me in such a logical sequence and in such a confrontative form as, helping to accustom the reader automatically to active mentation and contributing to an easy and simultaneous theoretical assimilation of the very essence of the questions dealt with, should give the possibility to cognize, first of all, not only with one's ordinary automatic consciousness, which in this case has no value, but with all one's being, that which is most important and is unfailingly required for the possibility of further work upon oneself, namely, the ephemeral nature of former conceptions and understandings.

An all-round acquaintance with the contents of these three books is necessary also in order that when I personally, or the mentioned instructors, speak during our general meetings about some question which in the given moment is the center -of-gravity question, and speak about its details, we may, for the purpose of economizing time, simply refer to the corresponding chapter in this first series, and you, already having preliminary information about this, may easily assimilate what we shall subsequently develop in detail.

For example, intending in today's meeting to speak about a question which is based on data I have already more or less elucidated in the last chapter of the third book, namely in the chapter entitled "From the Author," the deliberations on the proposed question today should be as a continuation of this chapter.

Well, if you were all well-informed of its contents, then I could for the purpose of economizing time refer to the requisite passages, but now I shall be compelled to waste time on reading to your certain extracts.

In the present case, one requires chiefly the knowledge of that part of the last chapter called "The Addition," which I wrote after I had very definitely shown in this chapter the complete automatism of contemporary man and his complete nullity in respect to the "independent manifestation of his individuality."

Having said this, I asked my secretary to read the extracts to which I referred.

Word for word, the content of these extracts is as follows:

"Such is the ordinary average man, an unconscious slave of the whole service to all-universal purposes, which are alien to his own personal individuality.

"He may live through all his life as he arose and was crystallized thanks to all kinds of influences eventually forming the conditions of life around him, and as such after death be destroyed forever.

"And although this is the lot of every life, yet at the same time Great Nature gave to some lives, as in the given case, to man, corresponding possibilities to be not merely a blind tool of the whole entire service to the all-universal aim but at the same time, serving Nature and actualizing consciously what is predetermined for him, to produce what is required in excess and to utilize this excess for his 'egoism,' that is to say, for the definition and manifestation of his own individuality.

"This possibility is given also for serving the common aim, as for the equilibrium of these objective laws such relatively liberated, self-constructed, independent lives, and in particular of human origin, are also necessary.

"Speaking thus about it, I consider it my moral duty here to add and particularly to underline that, although the said liberation is possible for man, not every man has a chance to attain it. There are a great many causes which do not permit it and which in most cases depend neither upon us personally nor upon great cosmic laws, but only upon various accidental conditions of our arising and formation, among which the chief are of course heredity and the conditions under which the process of our 'preparatory age' flows. It is just these uncontrollable conditions which may not permit this liberation. . .."

Stopping the reader at this point, I explained that of the contents of the subsequent few pages, omitted for the purpose of saving time, it is only necessary for the theme of this evening to know about the comparison which I had made there between human life as a whole and the flow of a big river forking at a certain place corresponding, according to my definition, to the time of man's reaching responsible age, that is, that age when it becomes definite in a man whether he has succeeded by that time in acquiring data for possessing his own I into two streams, one of which flows into the limitless ocean for subsequent movement evolutionary for itself, and the other into the nether regions for subsequent but evolutionary movement, in this case only for the needs of nature. Then I pointed out the place from which the reading should in the present case be continued.

"For us contemporary people," continued to read the secretary, "the chief evil is that on reaching responsible age we acquire, thanks to the various conditions of our ordinary existence established by us ourselves, chiefly in consequence of the abnormal what is called 'education' a common presence corresponding only to that stream of the river of life which ultimately empties itself into the 'nether regions,' and, entering it, we remain passive and, without reflecting about the consequences of this state, submit to the flow and drift on and on.

"As long as we remain passive, we shall have in the course of our further existence to submit slavishly to every caprice of all sorts of blind events and as a result inevitably shall serve solely as means for Nature's 'evolutionary and evolutionary constructions.'

"As most of you present here and listening to my explanations have already, as is said, 'crossed over' into responsible age and after my explanations sincerely cognize that until now you have not acquired your own I, and at the same time, according to the essence of all that I have said here, you have not pictured for yourselves any particularly agreeable perspectives, then, in order that you just you who have cognized this should not be greatly, as is said, 'disheartened' and should not fall into the so-called 'pessimism' prevalent everywhere in the contemporary abnormal life of people, I say quite sincerely, without any *arrière-pensée,* that, according to my convictions which have been formed thanks to long years of investigations, strengthened by numerous quite exceptionally conducted experiments on the results of which is based the 'Institute for the Harmonious Development of Man' founded by me even for you, everything is not yet lost.

"My special investigations and experimentally statistical elucidations on this subject showed me clearly and very definitely that by Great, All-solicitous Mother Nature the possibility is also foreseen for beings to acquire the kernel of their essence, that is to say, their own I, even after entering into responsible age.

"The foresight of Equitable Nature consists in the given case in this, that the possibility is given to us after our completed formation into responsible life, by our own intentions through certain inner experiencing's and certain outer conditions to crystallize in our common presence data for the obtaining of such a kernel of course with greater difficulty than in preparatory age.

"The process of intentional formation in one's presence of such data is conditioned by the difficulties of crossing over from one stream of the river of life to the other.

"It is interesting to note here that the expression often used by contemporary people, of course quite automatically, without any understanding of its hidden sense 'the first liberation of man' signifies, according to the interpretation of initiates of one school existing presently in Central Asia, just that supposed figurative understanding which I in my writings formulated as the possibility for each drop of water of the prime general river to cross from the stream which is predetermined to disappear into the 'nether regions' into the stream which empties itself into the vast space of the boundless ocean.

"As to the possibility of this crossing for a man who in his responsible age has already entered into the stream of the 'nether region,' although it is given by Great Nature, I must warn you, in order not to provoke in you so to say 'light-hearted illusions' regarding this possibility to cross from one stream to another, that it is not so easy merely to wish and you cross.

"For this it is indispensable, with a constantly active consciousness, first of all with extremely great intensity to obtain the intentional crystallization in oneself of the data for engendering in one's common presence an unquenchable impulse of desire for such a crossing, and then will follow a long inner struggle, requiring great tension of all the inner forces, with the obvious abnormalities crystallized in one's individuality and evident even to one's own self-reasoning, that is to say, a struggle with the crystallized habits unworthy for man even in his own understanding in a period of repose, which contribute, first, to the arising in us of our inner 'Evil-God' and second, to the supporting and increasing in us of its power and strength always and in everything, namely that 'Evil-God,' the presence of which creates ideal conditions, especially in contemporary people, for enjoying a state of 'immutable peace' speaking shortly, there will be required all kinds of corresponding, very complicated and difficult preparations. . .."

At this point, interrupting the reader again, I continued thus:

From the contents of the fragment which has just been read, each of you should already at least understand that the indispensable condition which is first of all required from a man for his still possible arrival on a new path, namely, the path of "evolutionary movement," is to have at least some data for the acquisition of his own I.

In the case of a man in whom, because of the conditions of his preparatory age, the time preordained by Nature for the purpose of the natural crystallization in his common presence of data for possessing in responsible age his own I has not been made use of, then, if in responsible age, when in general sane reasoning can sometimes be lawfully manifested in man, he accidentally grasps this fact and resolves to attain the possibility to be such as he ought to be in reality, namely, to have his own individuality conditioned by the unquestionable possession of his own I, he must for this purpose, first of all, unfailingly and consciously begin to crystallize in himself seven data as was established by really wise people of all ancient epochs specially inherent only in man, data which have for the quality of manifestation a reciprocal action between themselves in complete accordance with the fundamental law of the World, the sacred Heptaparaparshinokh.

Today I shall speak about only three of these seven psychic factors proper to man alone.

In the general psychic functioning of man, in certain automatically formed or intentionally created conditions depending upon mental associations and feeling-experiencing's, these three factors engender in the general presence of man three definite impulses.

Before continuing to explain just what is necessary and how one must consciously, both inwardly and outwardly, manifest oneself in order to obtain the arising in oneself of such data inherent only in man, which ought also to appear as lawful aspects of the whole individuality of a real man, I shall be compelled, on account of the absence in the English language of any exact verbal designation of these three impulses, and as a consequence the absence of an approximate under-standing of them, to waste my time, in order to give you an approximate understanding of them and choose for them some more or less corresponding conventional names which we shall use in our subsequent talks.

For an approximate definition of the first of these three human impulses which must arise and manifest themselves in a real man, one might employ the English word "can," yet not in the sense in which this word is used in the contemporary English language but in the sense in which Englishmen used it before what is called the "Shakespearean epoch."

Although for the exact definition of the second of these human impulses in the contemporary English language there is a word, namely "wish," it is nevertheless employed by you Americans, as well as by the English people themselves, only in order to vary, of course unconsciously, the degree of the expression of that so to say "slavish impulse" for which there are, particularly in this language, a multitude of words as, for example, "like," "want," "need," "desire" and so on.

And as regards a word for the expression and understanding of the third definite aforementioned human impulse, in the whole lexicon of words in the English language there cannot be found one even approximately corresponding.

This impulse, proper exclusively to man, can be denned in the English language only descriptively, that is, with many words. I should define it for now in the following words:

"The entire sensing of the whole of oneself."

This third impulse, which should be sometimes in the waking state of man, one of certain definite manifestations in the general presence of every normal man, is of all the seven exclusively proper to man impulses the most important, because its association with the first two, namely, those which I have already said can be approximately expressed in English by the words "can" and "wish," almost composes and represents the genuine I of a man who has reached responsible age.

It is only in a man with such an I that these three impulses, two of which are approximately defined in English by the words "I can" and "I wish," acquire in their turn that significance which I presume; which significance, and the corresponding force of action from their manifestation, is obtained only in a man who by his intentional efforts obtains the arising in himself of data for engendering these impulses sacred for man.

Only such a man, when he consciously says "I am" he really is; "I can" he really can; "I wish" he really wishes.

When "I wish" I feel with my whole being that I wish and can wish. This does not mean that I want, that I need, that I like or, lastly, that I desire. No. "I wish." I never like, never want, I do not desire anything, and I do not need anything all this is slavery; if "I wish" something, I must like it, even if I do not like it. I can wish to like it, because "I can."

I wish, I feel with my whole body that I wish.

I wish, because I can wish.

Based on my own experience, I consider it absolutely necessary to note here that the difficulty of a clear understanding of all this without a long and deep reflection and, in general, the complication of the process of standing on the right path for the obtaining in one's common presence of factors for engendering even only these first three, from the number of seven, impulses characterizing genuine man, derives, from the very first attempts, from the fact that, on the one hand, these impulses can exist almost exclusively when one has one's own genuine I and, on the other hand, the I can be in man almost exclusively when he has in him these three impulses.

For the conscious developing in oneself of the given impulses inherent only in man, I intend to recommend to you some of those simple exercises which were also previously presented in detail in the program of the Institute founded by me and were to be explained to the pupils who reached the mesoteric group.

I said "simple" because in various serious schools, existing even in present times, for the self-perfecting of man, there are for the same purpose very complicated exercises.

For a real influencing of the common presence of those who do all these special exercises, and for an easier assimilation of what is required and necessary, you must know first of all that the obtained totality of results of various functions proceeding in the psychic life of people, which is called "attention," is itself split automatically by the accidental surrounding conditions, as well as by an intentional force of will, into several definite parts, and each of these parts may be, of course also by itself as well as intentionally, concentrated on something special with a definite intensity

For the given case, it is indispensable first to learn to divide one's entire attention in three approximately equal parts, and to concentrate each separate part simultaneously for a definite time on three diverse inner or outer "objects."

For the possibility of a practical achieving of this aim, in the same mentioned detailed program were indicated a series of exercises under the name of "soil preparing."

Although the exercises indicated in the circumstantial program were intentionally composed in sequence and it was required to begin from number one, yet for you Americans in general, on account of several misunderstandings in the past, I consider it most useful to start from number four.

This exercise number four, from the series for preparing the soil, is performed in reality thus:

First, all one's attention must be divided approximately into three equal parts; each of these parts must be concentrated on one of the three fingers of the right or the left hand, for instance the forefinger, the third and the fourth, constating in one finger the result proceeding in it of the organic process called "sensing," in another the result of the process called "feeling," and with the third making any rhythmical movement and at the same time automatically conducting with the flowing of mental association a sequential or varied manner of counting.

Here there again arises the question of the poverty of the English language, this time in the sense that the contemporary people belonging to the English race and you Americans also, who have borrowed their language and use it in your ordinary life, totally lack any understanding of the difference between two entirely distinct impulses of an average man, namely, between the impulse of "feeling" and that of "sensing."

Since an understanding of this difference between these two impulses is very important for my subsequent indications concerning all the exercises required for you, as well as concerning the real nature of the psyche of man, I shall be compelled once more to interrupt the logical sequence of the elucidation of the theme I have begun and again waste my time on explaining, if only approximately for the present, this unexpectedly arisen philologically psychic question.

In order to explain to you this very important question, the difference between "sensing" and "feeling," I shall give you a corresponding definition.

A man "feels" when what are called the "initiative factors" issue from one of the dispersed localizations of his common presence which in contemporary science are called the "sympathetic nerve nodes," the chief agglomeration of which is known by the name of "solar plexus" and the whole totality of which functioning, in the terminology long ago established by me, is called the "feeling center"; and he "senses" when the basis of his "initiative factors" is the totality of what are called "the motor nerve nodes" of the spinal and partly of the head brain, which is called according to this terminology of mine the "moving center."

Just this difference in the nature of these two unknowns to your independent sources constitutes the difference in functions which you do not distinguish.

For this fourth preparatory exercise explained by me today, first of all it is necessary to learn with what exists in you now only as a substitute, so to say "fulfilling the obligation" of what should, in real man, be "self-willed attention" and in you is merely a "self-tenseness," simultaneously to observe three heterogeneous results proceeding in you, each coming from different sources of the general functioning of your whole presence: namely, one part of this attention of yours should be occupied with the constatation of the proceeding in one finger process of "sensing," another with the constatation of the proceeding in another finger process of "feeling," and the third part should follow the counting of the automatic movement of the third finger.

Although this fourth exercise is the most difficult of all the number of exercises composing this series, yet, in the given case, as I have said, on account of various misunderstandings, for you, in my opinion, only this exercise may on the one hand correct your errors of the past, and on the other hand prepare all that is required for the future.

And for cognizing its importance and indispensability for you, as well as its real difficulty, it is necessary to do it many,

many times. At the beginning you must try all the time only to understand the sense and significance of this exercise, without expecting to obtain any concrete result.

As only an all-round understanding of the sense and significance of this fourth and for you, first exercise, as well as the ability to carry it out, will perforce make it easier for you to cognize the sense and significance, as well as the carrying out, of all the subsequent exercises which are required for the acquisition of one's own individuality, I therefore advise you, so to say, to "mobilize" all your forces and possibilities, in order that you should "BE ABLE" for a definite time not to be lazy and at the same time to be, in relation to yourself, that is to say, to your weaknesses, quite merciless, because upon this first exercise depends your whole subsequent normal life, and all your future possibilities, inherent only in man, according to law.

And so, if you really wish to have in yourself that which alone can distinguish a man from an ordinary animal, that is to say, if you wish to be really such a one to whom Great Nature has given the possibility with the desire, that is, with a desire issuing from all the three separate spiritualized parts and with the conscious striving to transform yourself into a so to say "cultivated soil" for the germination and growth of that upon which lay the hopes and expectations of the CREATOR OF EVERYTHING EXISTING, then you must always and in everything, struggling with the weaknesses that are in you according to law, attain at any cost, first of all, an all-round understanding, and then the practical realization in your presence, of this exercise just elucidated by me, in order to have the chance for a conscious crystallizing in yourself of the data still engendering the three mentioned impulses which must be present obligatorily in the common presence of every man who has the right to call himself a GODLIKE CREATURE.

———

FOURTH TALK

*delivered by me on December 12th, 1930, at a meeting
of a newly formed group, to which were again admitted
the members of the so-called Orage group. The place
was crowded in the extreme.*

I want before beginning to expound the quintessence of this fourth talk of mine to describe, and even, if possible, with real picturing, several events which took place then among the members of this Orage group, after I proposed to them to sign the "receipt obligation" mentioned in a previous chapter.

I want to describe these events and the different consequences deriving from them which unexpectedly engendered even for myself very profitably arranged circumstances chiefly because, throwing a real, and not a puffing, light on it, as is the habit regarding everything American, one might give for the inner sight of every reader a very good picture for the understanding of how strongly is developed in these Americans, considered all over the Earth among contemporary people as the most cultured, the feeling which is called "herd instinct," which has become an infallible inherency of con- temporary people in general and is manifested in the fact that a man does not guide himself in his acts by his own reasoning but follows blindly the example of others, and how the degree of development of his mentation in the sense of his ableness to make logical confrontations is really of a very low level. I wish also to show that, thanks to these descriptions of mine, there will be elucidated and will become really clear for every reader of my writings at least that side of the custom, existing in the process of our common life, which is spread everywhere, especially among Americans, and consists in that people, in their striving to achieve the same aim, are divided into various so-called "parties" which, in my opinion, especially in these last years, have assumed the character of one of the biggest so to say "plagues" of our contemporary common life.

These events, which by their content can correspond also to the aim which I put to myself in exposing this series that is to say, that they might also carry an instructive character-proceeded in the following sequence:

After I had announced at the general meeting the indispensability of signing the mentioned obligation and had set a definite time by which it had to be signed, they almost all in the same evening, as I learned afterwards, dividing into separate groups, first walked about the streets and then, taking themselves off to various nocturnal "Childses," as they call them, or to the apartments of those whose what is called "domestic tyrant," usual in every contemporary household, was on that day absent, discussed and argued excitedly almost till morning as to what they should do.

On the next day, from the early morning, also meeting and talking by telephone with those of their comrades who had not been present at this general meeting, they continued their exchange of thoughts and opinions, and as a result of all these discussions and deliberations of theirs there were formed by that same evening three independent parties with various attitudes toward everything that had occurred.

The first party consisted of those who decided not only to sign the obligation required by me but also in the future unconditionally to fulfill all kinds of orders and indications issued exclusively only by me personally.

The second consisted of those in the psyche of whom through incomprehensible, at least to my mind, causes there was formed in this short time for some reason a strange factor, bidding their whole peculiar individuality not to recognize anything whatsoever issuing from me, but to remain true to the one who for several years had been for them, as one of them expressed himself, "not only teacher and mentor but also, as it were, their own 'loving father,' " that is to say, Mr. Orage.

The third party consisted of those who postponed their decision, awaiting the reply to the telegram they had sent to Mr. Orage asking what they should do.

All of those who joined the first party had to the last man signed the obligation before the appointed time was up.

In the psyche of those composing the second party, as it subsequently became clear, the mentioned strange factor progressively increased in its force up to the moment when the time appointed for the signing of the obligation had elapsed, and reached such a point that every one of them, in his so to say "belligerent animation" and fury in the fight with me, would have gone "a dozen better" than the famous ancient Balshakarians protecting their idol "Tantsatrata" from the devils specially sent to them from Hell.

And as regards those of my charming "dainty" American followers of my ideas who then made up the third party, it is just they who have shown and proved the degree of contemporary development of the logical mentation of people of their grouping, which is considered in contemporary life everywhere on Earth as one of the most civilized.

The various shades of complicated, fine and clever results of manifestation of this "logical mentation" of theirs then became really evident to all around them, and particularly to me, from the fact that, having received the news of the arrival soon of Mr. Orage himself on the field of action, as he was already on his way, they began to invent all kinds of "crafty" circumstances supposedly independent of them, and began to bring these "ideally well" invented circumstances of theirs to the attention of my poor secretary, and did this moreover not themselves but through others by telephone.

All this they did for the purpose of putting off their final decision until the arrival of Mr. Orage, preparing thus at all events a respectable justification for not signing the obligation at the proper time.

Two days before the fourth general meeting of this group reorganized by me on new principles, Mr. Orage himself arrived finally in New York, already informed about everything that had taken place here in his absence.

On the very day of his arrival, he requested through my secretary a personal interview with me.

I confess that I did not expect this because, as it was known to me, many of the members of the group had written to him about all that had happened here and particularly, of course, about my reiterated not very flattering opinion of him.

At first, I wanted to answer to his request that I could meet him with pleasure as an old friend, but on one express condition, that there would not be any talk about all kinds of misunderstandings nor of various new statements I had made during his absence in the presence of people who were members of his group, but all at once, remembering the alarming news received by me one hour ago of the bad turn of my material affairs connected with the liquidation of goods brought by my companions, I decided to delay the answer in order to think it over well, because at the same time a thought germinated in me: would it not be possible to use such a request to me for my aims, considering that my prime decision not to utilize the members of this group for the actualization of the purpose of this trip of mine had by this time already been changed in consequence of the manifestations of some of them, manifestations quite intolerable and unworthy of people who had already been for several years in contact with my ideas, especially since it seemed that they had been thinking about them and had understood them well.

Thinking over and confronting all kinds of results which might arise in various cases, I decided to answer him through the same secretary of mine as follows:

"Most calm, most promising and particularly most esteemed by me

Mr. Orage:

"After everything that has happened here, as much as you know me, I have no more the right to meet you on the former conditions, even merely as an old friend!

"Now, without breaking my principles, most of which are known to you, I can meet you and even, as in the past, occupy myself with the process of 'pouring from the empty into the void' exclusively if you also, Mr. Orage, will sign the obligation I proposed to all the members of the group you have directed."

Having received this answer, Mr. Orage, to the great astonishment of the people near me who had journeyed with me, came at once to that flat of mine where some of the people lived who came with me, among whom was my secretary, and first of all, without arguing, signed the obligation; then, evidently copying as it was related to me my usual attitude when I am sitting, he began to speak calmly as follows:

"Knowing well," he said, "of course thanks to Mr. Gurdjieff, the difference between the manifestations of a man engendered by his real nature, which is the pure result of his heredity and education in his childhood, and the manifestations engendered by his 'automatic mentation' which, as he himself defines it, is a mere result of all kinds of accidental impressions assimilated without any order, and, being at the same time well-informed by letters mostly sent to me by various members of the group here about everything that has taken place here in my absence, I at once understood, without any doubt whatsoever, what was hidden behind the proposal made to me by Mr. Gurdjieff, which at first glance seemed really absurd, a proposal to me to sign also, like the others, the obligation which would deprive me of the right to have any relationship not only with the members of that group which I directed for such a long time but, however strange it may sound, even with myself.

"I understood it at once, obviously because during these last days I meditated very much regarding the lack of correspondence between my inner conviction and what Mr. Gurdjieff calls 'my playing a role here,' and the heavy, unpleasant feeling created in me by the sincere cognition of that lack always increased more and more.

"In my moments of a quiet state, especially during the last year, I often confessed inertly with sincerity the contradiction of my outer manifestations with the ideas of Mr. Gurdjieff and, therefore, the maleficence of my verbal influence on people whom I guided so to say in accordance with his ideas.

"Frankly speaking, almost all the impressions received from what Mr. Gurdjieff has said here in the general meetings and to individual members of our group about me and my activity exactly correspond to my inner conviction.

"Many times, did I intend, myself, to put a stop to such a

double manifestation of myself, but various life circumstances constantly prevented me from setting out to do so with the requisite decisiveness.

"Having received from him now," he continued, "at first glance an absurd proposal, but knowing the habit of my Teacher 'always to keep deep thoughts under ordinary so to say meaningless outer expressions,' I, having thought only a moment, clearly understood that if I do not profit from the opportunity to rid myself now forever of such, as I should say, 'double-dealing' of mine, I should never be able to do it again.

"I decided therefore to begin by signing the obligation required by Mr. Gurdjieff, and at the same time I give my word in your presence that, from this moment on, I shall not have any further communication either with any of the members of the former group, or even with my former self, on the grounds of the former conditions of mutual relations and influences.

"I wish very much, of course if Mr. Gurdjieff permits, to become from this day an ordinary member of this now reorganized new group."

Such a philosophizing of Mr. Orage made such a strong impression on me and produced such a strange reaction in my peculiar psyche that now, even with the strongest desire, I cannot refrain from relating this and describing in the style of my former teacher, now almost a Saint, Mullah Nasiruddin, the surroundings and the conditions in which proceeded the process of assimilation in my Being of the so to say "tzimmes" of the above-mentioned philosophizing of my dear "Anglo-American *délicatesse* Mr. Orage, who was during many years in America almost the chief representative and interpreter of my ideas.

When they told me of his having come and of his philosophizing concerning the proposal I made him, and his decision also to sign this obligation, I was in the kitchen, preparing the so to say "gravity center dish," as it is called by my "drones," which I did every day during my stay in New York for the purpose chiefly of having some physical exercise, devoting each day, moreover, to the preparation of a new national dish of some one of the peoples inhabiting all continents.

That day I was preparing the favorite dish of the people inhabiting the space between China and Russian Turkestan.

At the moment when there was reported to me the arrival of Mr. Orage and of his fine philosophical deliberations, I was beating the yolks of eggs with cinnamon and pompadory.

And when the outer sounding of certain of the sentences used by him began to be perceived in me nobody knows why right in the center between the two hemispheres of the brain, in all that totality of the functioning of my organism which in general engenders in man "feeling," there gradually began a process similar to the experiencing of a feeling called a "touchy emotion," and I suddenly, without any consideration, instead of a pinch of ginger, dumped into the casserole with the left hand the whole supply in the kitchen of powdered cayenne pepper, an action which is not at all proper to me during such a, for me, sacred ritual as the composition and preparation for obtaining a corresponding symphonic taste of some dish which has existed on the Earth since olden times; and, swinging my right arm in rhythm with all my force, "dealt a blow on the back" to my poor secretary of music, who was there in the kitchen washing dishes, and then flung myself into my room, fell on the sofa and, burying my head in the cushions which, by the way, were half moth-eaten, began to sob with bitter tears.

I continued to sob, of course with no reasonable motive, but only seized by the fully possessing me and by inertia continuing mentioned feeling of emotion until my friend the doctor, who had accompanied me to America, having by chance noticed the beginning of a psychic state as yet unknown to him, came into the room with a big bottle of Scotch whisky specially made for Americans. After I had swallowed this medical remedy of his, though physically I calmed down a little, the twitching which had begun in the left half of my body continued until suppertime, namely, until the moment when I and all the people who were with me were compelled, for lack of any other food, to eat the dish I had so immoderately peppered.

What experience began in me and what results settled in my consciousness from the associations proceeding in my mentation thanks to this immoderately peppered dish, I shall not describe in this place of my writings because the idea has just arisen in me of making this information the issuing-basis for a certain highly edifyingly instructive question on the psyche of contemporary man, born and bred on the continent of Europe, which I propose to elucidate from every aspect in one of the following books of this third series of my writings.

Regarding how I utilized for my, in the objective sense, equitable aims the manifestations in the given case of the mentation, developed to the highest degree of contemporary civilization, of these so to say representatives of Americans, this will be shown by the following:

When, on the day after Mr. Orage's visit, I began to receive from early hours in the morning numerous requests from his adepts, almost entreating me to enroll them as members of this new group, I gave the order to answer to all of them as follows:

"To the next general meeting of the newly organized group, any former member of the Orage group can be admitted on the two following conditions.

"The first condition is to pay a fine, for not having signed the obligation in time, of a sum of dollars corresponding to the material possibilities of the given person, which will be established by a committee, specially chosen for this purpose, of several members of the former group.

"The second condition is that all those who have fulfilled the first condition, that is, the immediate payment of the fine imposed on them which will not in any circumstances be returned, will be enrolled for the time being only as candidates for the new group, and only after a certain established term will it be decided, depending on the fulfillment or nonfulfillment by them of subsequent conditions, who is worthy to remain in the group as a full member and who is unconditionally to leave the group."

On the same day, a committee was formed by my choice of four members who, together with me, established seven gradations of fines.

The first and highest fine was fixed at the sum of $3, 648, the second at $1, 824, the third at $912, the fourth at $456, the fifth at $228, the sixth at $114 and the last and lowest at $57.

To the sum total of these fines were added the charges which I fixed for shorthand copies of the talks I delivered at the first three meetings of the new exoteric group to those who had been absent, indispensable for the understanding of my subsequent talks: from the first group, that is to say, those who unconditionally signed the obligation $10; from those who belonged to the second group, that is to say, who did not recognize anything whatsoever issuing from me $40 and those who had belonged to the third group, that is, those who decided to await the arrival of Mr. Orage $20.

All that made a total of $113, 000, which sum I divided into two equal parts, one of which I kept myself, and the other for the beginning of the formation of a fund for mutual aid to the materially needy members of this first exoteric group organized by me, a group for collective self-perfecting with a program drawn up already in exact accordance with my ideas.

Thus, my delivery of the said fourth talk, the summarized contents of which I now wish to cite, took place this time in the presence of Mr. Orage himself and of several of his former so to say "first-rank" defenders now sitting, of course, with "tails between their legs" and facial expressions of unchangeable "plasto-oleaginous" traits.

That evening, after the demonstration of the music usually composed the day before and after the performance, according to the established custom, by my secretary of music, and at the choice and wish of the majority present, of two pieces of the former series of my music, I began thus:

"According to all kinds of historical data and to sane logical human mentation, man, as compared to the other external forms of life arising and existing on Earth, both by bodily organization, as well as the degree of complexity of the form of functioning of his psyche for every kind of perceiving and manifestation, ought to be, among these other external forms of life, really supreme and so to say 'directive' in respect of regulating the correctness of ordinary life, as well as in respect of giving indications for the worthy justification of the sense and aim of his existence in the process of the actualization of what is foreordained by our Common Father.

"In the general process of the variform life on the Earth, as these same historical data show us, it was thus at the beginning, and only afterwards, when there arose in the psyche of people chiefly owing to their vice called laziness and with each generation there began to increase in the intensity of its action on their common presence that 'something' which automatically enjoins this common presence of theirs constantly to desire and to strive to attain peace, from then on, with the increasing in man of the intensity of the action of this fundamental evil of theirs, there began proportionately also to increase their removal from the general life proceeding on Earth.

"As the correctness of the functioning proceeding in us of any relatively independent organ depends on the correctness of the tempo of the general functioning of the whole organism, so also the correctness of our life depends on the correctness of the automatic life of all the other external forms of life arising and existing together with us on our planet.

"As the general tempo of life on the Earth engendered by the cosmic laws consists of the totality of all the tempos both of our human life and also of all the other external forms of life, therefore, the abnormalities of the tempo of any one form of life, or even only the disharmony, must inevitably evoke abnormality and disharmony in another form of life.

"I began to speak about such an abstract theme, at first glance distant from the one put by me for your immediate interest, chiefly because, wishing today to explain to you the method of one so to say 'cardinal' exercise for the conscious crystallization in you of the first of the seven psychic data, inherent only in man, I wish to give you the information about such an aspect of the objective truth for the precise and broad understanding of which it is indispensable to make such a digression of general character.

"I consider it important and for you very useful to note that such an aspect of objective truth in the process of human life was always, since ancient times on Earth, one of the fundamental secrets of initiates of all epochs and ranks, and the knowledge of it, as it is already established, might contribute by itself to increase the intensity of assimilation of the results deriving from this first, as well as other similar exercises.

"I wish to explain to you just about that totality of cosmic substances and properties inherent to the totality which, not only in our human life but also in the other external forms of life, is the chief actualizing factor, and which, being the 'second substantial food,' is nothing other than the 'air' we breathe.

"The air, from which are eliminated the elements necessary for our life, to be transformed afterwards in our organism into other cosmic substances for the needs of the general universal actualization, like every definite cosmic concentration is composed of two kinds of active elements with two properties, quite contradictory in their totality.

"One kind of active element has a subjective process of evolutionary striving, and the other, of involutionary.

"The air, like every definite cosmic concentration, formed owing to all kinds of common-cosmic laws and to various ensuing secondary laws depending upon the position and the reciprocal action, as in the given case of our planet, with the other large cosmic concentrations of the totality of substances, acquires and possesses a multitude of specific particularities.

"From among this multitude of particularities, we, for the present case, must know about that one which since long ago has in the process of human life always been one of the chief secrets of all ranks of initiates of all epochs.

"This particularity is that. ..."

FIFTH TALK

to the same group on December 19th, 1930

I began as follows:

Before questioning you, according to the usage established by me, in order to better orient myself for giving further indications as now, for example, questioning you about why and how, as a result of your "spare time" reflections during the past week, you have elucidated and understood my indications concerning the first exercise which I recommended at the third meeting for the purpose of preparing in your common presences "fertile soil" for the possibility of intentionally composing data for the impulses sacred for man, 1 find it necessary to indicate to you two other independent exercises which were in the general program of the Institute founded by me, but which belonged to quite a different series of exercises, which were then also, for a definite category of pupils, one of what are called "assisting means" for acquiring one's own real I.

Besides these exercises of which I now speak and also the information about them into which I now wish to initiate you, being for you a really good means for this aim, they will help you firstly to apprehend and understand many details of the significance and sense of the first of the seven what are called "cardinal" exercises I mentioned, and secondly, you will, thanks to this information, learn, by the way, of two definite notions which from the dawn of centuries among all categories of initiated persons on the Earth have been considered and are at the present time considered "secret," and an acquaintance with which for the average man can, according to the convictions of these initiates, even prove ruinous.

You must here know that on the Earth, in almost all epochs, the persons who deserved to become genuine initiates were divided into three categories.

The initiates belonging to the first category were those who thanks to their intentional sufferings and conscious labors attained a high gradation of what is called Being, and for this they acquired the title "Saint." To the second category belonged those who thanks to the same factors acquired a great deal of all kinds of information, and to their names was added the title "Learned"; and to the third category, those who by means of again the same factors attained Being and also enlightened themselves concerning a great number of objective truths, and to their names was added the title "Sage."

The first of the aforementioned secrets is that as a means for self-perfecting a man can use a certain property which is in his psyche, and which is even of a very negative character. This property can serve as an aid to self-perfecting and exists in people in general, particularly in contemporary people, and especially in you, and is none other than that which I have many times condemned and which people themselves consider an unworthy manifestation for a man who has reached responsible age of course in this respect also excluding themselves and it is called "self-deception."

Such an, at first glance, illogicality and deduction not

corresponding to any human sane reasoning, namely, that such a property unbecoming to the psyche of a man of adult age can consciously be made use of for such an immeasurably high aim, is obtained owing to the fact that the cognizance of truths concerning the possibilities of self-perfection, and the real forming in oneself of what is required for this, must proceed not in the ordinary consciousness of a man, which for the given case has almost no significance, but in what is called the subconscious, and since, thanks to all kinds of accidents ensuing from the various abnormalities of our ordinary life, it has become impossible for a man, particularly for a contemporary man, to take in anything at all and so to say "digest" it directly with his subconsciousness, therefore it is necessary for him, as has in the course of many centuries been experimentally proven by persons of Pure Reason, to use a special means for inculcating in his subconsciousness some reasonable indication accidentally grasped by his ordinary consciousness and not contradictory to his instinct, and this can be done only by means of this self-deceptive imaginativeness inherent in him.

If you have understood without any doubt what you must do, and how, and fully hope at some time to attain this in reality, you must at the beginning often imagine, but imagine only, that this is already present in you.

This is necessary chiefly in order that the consciousness forming in oneself during an active state should continue also during a passive state.

For the correct understanding of the significance of this first assisting exercise, it is first of all necessary to know that when a normal man, that is, a man who already has his real I, his will, and all the other properties of a real man, pronounces aloud or to himself the words "I am," then there always proceeds in him, in his, as it is called, "solar plexus," so to say "reverberation," that is, something like a vibration, a feeling, or something of the sort.

This kind of reverberation can proceed also in other parts of his body in general, but only on the condition that, when pronouncing these words, his attention is intentionally concentrated on them.

If the ordinary man, not having as yet in himself data for the natural reverberation but knowing of the existence of this fact, will, with conscious striving for the formation in himself of the genuine data which should be in the common presence of a real man, correctly and frequently pronounce these same and for him as yet empty words, and will imagine that this same reverberation proceeds in him, he may thereby ultimately through frequent repetition gradually acquire in himself as to say theoretical "beginning" for the possibility of a real practical forming in himself of these data.

He who is exercising himself with this must at the beginning, when pronouncing the words "I am," imagine that this same reverberation is already proceeding in his solar plexus.

Here, by the way, it is curious to notice that as a result of the intentional concentration of this reverberation on any part of his body, a man can stop any disharmony which has arisen in this said part of the body, that is to say, he can for example cure his headache by concentrating the reverberation on that part of the head where he has the sensation of pain.

At the beginning it is necessary to pronounce the words "I am" very often and to try always not to forget to have the said reverberation in one's solar plexus.

Without this even if only imagined experiencing of the reverberation, the pronouncing aloud or to oneself of the words "I am" will have no significance at all.

The result of the pronouncing of them without this reverberation will be the same as that which is obtained from the automatic associative mentation of man, namely, an increase of that in the atmosphere of our planet from our perception of which, and from its blending with our second food, there arises in us an irresistible urge to destroy the various tempos of our ordinary life somehow established through centuries.

This second exercise, as I have already said, is only preparatory and when you have acquired the knack, as it were, of experiencing this process imagined in yourself, only then will I give you further definite real indications for the actualization in yourself of real results.

First of all, concentrate the greater part of your attention on the words themselves, "I am," and the lesser part concentrate on the solar plexus, and the reverberation should gradually proceed of itself.

At first it is necessary to acquire only, so to say, the "taste" of these impulses which you have not as yet in you, and which for the present you may designate merely by the words "I am," "I can," "I wish."

I am, I can, I am can. I am, I

wish, I am wish.

In concluding my elucidations of this assisting exercise, I will once more repeat, but in another formulation, what I have already said.

If "I am," only then "I can"; if "I can," only then do I deserve and have the objective right to wish.

Without the ability to "can" there is no possibility of having anything; no, nor the right to it.

First, we must assimilate these expressions as external designations of these impulses in order ultimately to have the impulses themselves.

If you several times experience merely the sensation of what I have just called the "taste" of these impulses sacred for man, you will then already be indeed fortunate, because you will then feel the reality of the possibility of sometime acquiring in your presence data for these real Divine impulses proper only to man.

And on these Divine impulses there is based for humanity the entire sense of everything existing in the Universe, beginning from the atom, and ending with everything existing as a whole and, among other things, even your dollars.

For an all-round assimilation of both these "assisting" or as they might otherwise be called "helping" exercises for the mastering of the chief exercise, I now, at the very beginning of the formation of this new group composed of various persons pursuing one and the same aim, find it necessary to warn you of an indispensable condition for the successful attainment of this common aim, and that is in your mutual relations to be sincere.

The unconditional requirement of such sincerity among all kinds of other conditions existed, as it happened to become known to me from various authentic sources, among people of all past times and of every degree of intellectuality, whenever they gathered together for the collective attainment of some common aim.

In my opinion, it is only by fulfilling this condition for the given proposed collective work that it is possible to attain a real result in this aim which one has set oneself, and which has already become for contemporary people almost impossible.

Each of you having become an equal-rights participant in this group newly formed for the attainment of one and the same so to say "ideal" must always struggle with such impulses, inevitably arising in you and unworthy of man, as "self-love," "pride," "conceit" and so on, and not be ashamed to be sincere in your answers concerning your observations and constatations on the exercises recommended by me.

Any information expressed by any of you relating to the elucidation of the various details of this first exercise which is for all of you at the present moment the center of gravity, can be, in the collective work, of great value in helping one another.

In the present case, you must not be afraid of being sincere among yourselves.

Being occupied with the solution of questions concerning this common great aim, each of you must always cognize and instinctively feel that you are all in a certain respect similar to each other, and that the well-being of one of you depends on the well-being of the others.

No one of you separately is capable of doing anything real at all; therefore, even for the sake of only an egoistic aim, help one another in this newly formed group which might also be called a brotherhood. The more sincere you are with one another, the more useful you will be to one another.

Of course, be sincere only here in the group, and in questions concerning the common aim.

Sincerity with everyone in general is weakness, slavery and even a sign of hysteria.

Although the normal man must be able to be sincere, yet he must also know when, where and for what purpose it is necessary to be sincere.

And in the present case, to be sincere is desirable. Therefore, without restraint, speak of all the results attained by you from doing this kind of exercise.

I consider it necessary, before explaining these details, again to say a little about that specific totality of the results from the general functioning in the human psyche of what is called attention.

Although, in the normal man, this attention in the passive state is also a "something" of proportionately blended results of the corresponding actions of all the three independent automatized parts in his whole individuality, and is always one whole, yet in an active state such a man can consciously concentrate this whole attention of his on anything, either on some part of his common presence or on something outside him, in such a sop to say "collectiveness" that all the associations automatically proceeding in him, which being law-conformable results of the general functioning of his organism must always, as long as he breathes, inevitably proceed, will totally cease to hinder him.

Here it might as well be remarked that, according to authentic information which has reached us from the very ancient past, it is clearly stated that it was very definitely proved by learned persons then that these automatically flowing associations never cease while a man lives, and in certain people still continue to proceed after death for several days by momentum.

In speaking of these associations which automatically flow in man, I might as well, by the way, so to say, "illuminatingly clarify" yet another at first glance insignificant aspect of the phenomenal stupidity of people who believe and ascribe significance to all their foolish "dreams."

When a man really sleeps normally, his attention by the quality of which the so to say "gradation" of the difference between the waking state and sleep is conditioned also sleeps, that is to say, his attention is, according to the law-conformable inherencies in him, stored up with corresponding force for the subsequent necessary intensive manifestations.

But when owing to some disharmony in the general functioning of a man's organism, most often to a non-normal expenditure in his waking state of the law-conformably accumulated energy this part of the general psyche of his waking state is not capable of normally actualizing itself during sleep, then, from the associations flowing in him, constated with this attention so to say "a bit here and a bit there," these famous "dreams" are obtained, that is to say, human foolishness.

Secondly, a normal man can intentionally divide his whole attention, of which I have already spoken, into two or even three separate parts, and concentrate each of these on various independent objects inside or outside himself.

It will be very useful, in my opinion, for the productivity of the further work in this newly formed group of ours, if now, just before explaining to you the procedure of this second assisting exercise, I tell you also that, when I had drawn up the detailed plan for my Institute mentioned here many times, I was then already convinced of the impossibility of exactly explaining and fully formulating in words the various fine points of the procedures of any intentional experiencing's and exercises for the purpose of self-perfection, and, knowing at the same time of the existence among our remote ancestors of a special method which was then called the "principle of illustrative inculcation" for the purpose of better taking in new information, I therefore introduced this method also in the general program, and frequently employed it in certain circumstances; and now in view of the fact that I intend, after the work has begun in this newly formed group of followers of my ideas, also to employ this method, I therefore consider it expedient and opportune for the elucidations of the procedure of this second assisting exercise to keep partly to this, in my opinion, only true and useful method for such cases.

Well then, I am now sitting among you, as you see, and although I am looking at Mr. L. yet I am intentionally directing all my attention, which you are not able to see, on my foot, and consequently any manifestation Mr. L. produces within my field of vision I see only automatically my attention, which at the present moment is one whole, being in another place.

This whole attention of mine, I now intentionally divide into two equal parts.

The first half I consciously direct to the uninterrupted constatation and continuous sensing of the process proceeding in me of my breathing.

By means of this part of my attention I definitely feel that something takes place in me with the air I breathe.

I first clearly feel that, when I breathe in the air, the greater part, passing through my lungs, goes out again, and the lesser part remains and as it were settles there, and then I feel that this settled part is gradually penetrating inward and is as it were spreading through my whole organism.

In consequence of the fact that only a part of my attention is occupied with the observation of the process of breathing proceeding in me, all the mental, feeling, and reflex associations automatically flowing in my common presence still continue to be noticed by the free part of my attention and hinder that first part of my attention intentionally directed upon a definite object, but already to a much lesser extent.

Now I direct the second half of my attention to my head brain for the purpose of observing and possibly constating any process proceeding in it.

And already I am beginning to feel in it, from the totality of automatically flowing associations, the arising of something very fine, almost imperceptible to me.

I do not know just what this is, nor do I wish to know, but I definitely constate, feel and sense that this is some definite "something" arising from the process automatically proceeding in my head brain of associations of previously consciously perceived impressions.

While this second half of my attention is occupied with the aforesaid, the first half continues all the time uninterruptedly to watch, with so to say, "concentrated interest," the result proceeding from the process of my breathing.

I now consciously direct this second half of my attention and, uninterruptedly "remembering the whole of myself," I aid this something arising in my head brain to flow directly into my solar plexus. I feel how it flows. I no longer notice any automatic associations proceeding in me.

Having finished this so to say "monologue" of mine I continued to tell them, now in the usual way, the following:

In spite of the fact that I have done this exercise just now among you for the purpose of illustratively elucidating its details to you, and have in consequence done it under conditions not corresponding to the possibility of accumulating to the full in my common presence the entire beneficial result of this exercise, nevertheless, I now begin at the present moment to feel incomparably better than before beginning this demonstrational explanation.

Owing to my "solar plexus" intentionally and directly taking in the law conformable results of the air I was breathing and the results arising in my head brain of the previously consciously perceived impressions, I feel much more fully that "I am," "I can" and "I can wish."

But you, if you please, do not get too enthusiastic and too animated about my state which you vividly sense and which you also desire to acquire.

This for the time being cannot happen with any of you.

From this exercise of mine which I had to do here among you for the purpose of elucidation, there has been obtained in my common presence a result realistically sensed by all of you because I already have a fully denned subjective I, and the whole totality composing it is already more or less adapted for the results of corresponding impressions and law-conformable regulating.

And therefore, this I of mine absorbs this law-conformable food proper to it more intensively.

You, for the time being, must not expect such a definite result from your intentional repetitions of this same exercise.

Do not, for the time being, do this exercise in order to be strong; this also is for you only preparation for at some time having your own I, and at the same time for constating, with indubitable certitude, those two real sources from which this I can arise.

Now, without philosophizing and without your, for you, maleficent discussions, try first of all to understand the totality of all that I have said today, and then do the exercise for yourself, but without any hope or expectation of any definite results.

———————

THE OUTER AND INNER
WORLD OF MAN

Although the subject which I intend to elucidate by means of the text of this chapter of the last book of my writings is entirely lacking in the mentation of contemporary people, there nevertheless flows from the ignorance of the meaning of this subject the greatest part, if not all, of the misunderstandings which take place in the process of our common life.

Not only do the causes of almost all the misunderstandings of our common life flow from the lack of understanding of the significance of the given subject, but also exclusively in it are contained all the answers to the possibility of solving the chief problem of our existence.

That is, thanks alone to the recognition and all-round understanding of the sense and significance of this subject is it possible to solve the problem of the prolongation of human life.

Before beginning the further development of this question, I wish to cite the contents of an ancient manuscript with which I accidentally became acquainted in quite exceptional life circumstances.

This very ancient manuscript, the contents of which I intend to make use of, is one of those relics which is handed down from generation to generation by a very limited number of people, that is, by "Initiates" not such "initiates," however, as have been multiplying recently in Europe, but genuine ones.

In this case, by "Initiates" of an esoteric sect which still exists at the present time in one of the remote corners of Central Asia.

The text of this manuscript is expounded, as was done in antiquity, "podobolizovany," in the form of symbolizing, or, as it is called in esoteric science, "making alike," that is, allegorically quite different from the form now established for mentation among contemporary people.

As the difference between these forms is very well-known to me, of course also accidentally, I will endeavor to transmit the sense of this text as exactly as possible but in agreement with the form of mentation now established among contemporary people.

This ancient manuscript says the following:

> The general psyche of every man on reaching maturity, which begins on an average in the male sex at twenty years and in the female sex at the beginning of the thirteenth year, consists of three totalities of functioning which have almost nothing in common with each other.

> The course of action of all three of these independent totalities of functioning in the common presence of a man who has attained maturity takes place simultaneously and incessantly.

All the factors making up and producing these three totalities of functioning begin, and cease, to form in man at different periods of his life.

The factors producing in man the first totality of functioning, unless special measures are employed, are formed, as has been established long ago, only in childhood, in boys on an average until the age of eleven years, and in girls until the age of seven.

The factors producing the second totality of functioning begin to form in boys from the age of nine years, and in girls even from the age of four years, lasting in different cases a different length of time, approximately until the attainment of maturity.

And factors producing the third totality begin to form from the attainment of maturity, continuing in the average man at present only until the age of sixty, and in woman only until the age of forty-five.

But in the case of people who have consciously perfected themselves to the so-called "all-centers-awake state," that is, to the state of being able in their waking state to think and feel on their own initiative, these factors still continue to form in man until the age of three hundred years and in woman until the age of two hundred.

The forming of all the factors for the functioning's of these three entirely separate totalities of functioning proceeds in people in accordance also with the universal law of "three-foldness."

For the formation of factors of the first totality, there serve as the "anode beginning," on the one hand, all kinds of involuntarily perceived outer impressions and, on the other hand, impressions resulting from so-called "all-centered dozing"; and as the "cathode beginning" there serve the results of reflexes of the organism, chiefly of those organs having a hereditary particularity.

For the formation of the factors of the second totality, there serve as the "anode beginning" outer impressions taken in under a certain pressure and having thereby the character of being intentionally implanted from outside, and as the "cathode beginning" the results of the functioning of factors formed from impressions of a similar kind previously perceived.

The factors of the third totality of functioning's are formed from the results of "contemplation," that is, from results received from the "voluntary contact" of the factors of the first two totalities, for which moreover the results of the second totality serve as the "anode beginning" and the results of the first totality serve as the "cathode."

One of the properties of such an actualization of all three separate totalities of functioning's producing the general psyche of man is that which, by combinations of the "voluntary contact" of the actions of these three independent totalities of functioning, causes to proceed in one of them the impregnation of those processes proceeding in the other totalities, as well as those proceeding outside of the given man which happen to fall into the sphere of the subjective action of his organs of perception.

The pan of this property found in the common presence of man, ordinarily perceived by people, is that which is called "attention."

The degree of sensitivity of the manifestation of this property or, as otherwise denned by ancient science, "the strength of embrace" of this "attention" depends entirely upon the so-called "gradation of the total state" of a given man.

For the definition of this property in man, which is called "attention," there is, by the way, found also in ancient science the following verbal formulation:

"THE DEGREE OF BLENDING OF THAT WHICH IS THE SAME IN THE IMPULSES OF OBSERVATION AND CONSTATATION IN ONE TOTALITY'S

PROCESSES WITH THAT OCCURRING IN OTHER TOTALITIES."

This above-mentioned "gradation of the total state" of man extends, as science formulates it, from the strongest subjective intensity of "self-sensation" to the greatest established "self-losing."

That totality always becomes the initiating factor for the realization of a common function of the three separate totalities which represent the general psyche of man in which at the given moment this "gradation of the total state" has its center of gravity.

I have cited this at-first-glance fantastic hypothesis of our distant ancestors at the beginning of the illumination of the given question, first, because it can be a very good starting point for what follows, and second, because my own attempts to make clear to myself the true significance of just this hypothesis have led me to the conclusions which I wish to impart to my readers in the present chapter.

From the contents of this ancient "fantastic" scientific assumption, that which intrigued me personally, during the course of many years, was chiefly the mentioned verbal formulation, "The degree of blending of that which is the same in the impulses of observation and constatation in one totality's processes with that occurring in other totalities."

Though attaching great significance to everything else in this hypothesis, I could by no means understand the meaning expressed in this verbal formulation.

Especially was I intrigued by the words, "that which is the same." What is "sameness"? Why "sameness"? For what purpose this

peculiar "sameness"?

Even that idea, "absurd" for all contemporary scientists, that there proceed in man simultaneously three associations of independent nature, did not surprise me, and I accepted it with a feeling of great respect for the knowledge of ancient people.

And it did not surprise me because previously, at the time of my special verifications of what seemingly pertains to the psyche of man, carried out with the aid of all sorts of experimental means attained by contemporary civilization, chiefly by means of the science of "hypnotism," I noted and firmly established that there flow simultaneously in man three kinds of associations of thought, of feeling and of mechanical instinct.

Most important of all is that not only do the three kinds of independent associations flow simultaneously, but also there participate in all of them the results of the three sources found in man for the transformation of the three natures of so-called "cosmic vivifying-ness."

These sources are located in man as follows: the first, in a part of the brain, the second, in a part of the spinal column and the third, in a part of the solar plexus.

part of the brain, the second, in a part of the spinal column; and the third, in a part of the solar plexus.

These three kinds of associations in one man explain that peculiar sensation, noticed at times by everyone, as though there were several beings living in him. Those who wish to acquaint themselves more fully with these questions are advised to learn, that is, not simply to read but to immerse themselves in, that chapter of the first series of my writings entitled "The Holy Planet Purgatory."

On reading over what has just been written, there involuntarily arises in me the question as to which must appear to the reader more fantastic: that which I myself have written, or the hypothesis of our distant ancestors which I have cited.

It seems to me that every reader on first comparing them will find the one as bad as the other. A little later he will blame only me, that I, in spite of living in this period of civilization, should write such nonsense.

He will forgive the ancestors, however, as he is able to put himself into their position, and with the reason proper to him will argue approximately thus:

"How were they to blame that in their time our civilization had not yet existed? And once having become learned, they too had to occupy themselves with something. And for a fact, at that time, not one electrical machine existed, even of the simplest sort."

Not having been able to restrain myself, and once again having borne one of my weaknesses, consisting of in, as is said, "cracking a joke" at the most serious moments of my writings, I wish to take advantage of this incidental digression from the basic theme to describe a very peculiar coincidence which took place a few days ago, in connection with the writing of this last book of mine.

In connection with the writing of this book there have been, altogether, many coincidences, seemingly very strange at first glance, but which on closer scrutiny have shown themselves to be according to law.

Of course, I shall not write about all these coincidences, as this would not be possible, I would probably have to write ten other books.

However, for a better characterization of these strange coincidences and the consequences which have arisen from them, hindering the exposition of this book, I will depict, aside from the just mentioned one which happened the day before yesterday, also the first, which took place on November 6th,

1934, the first day of the recommencement of my writing.

As I have already said in the prologue, I decided, after a year's interruption in my writings, to begin to write again on the 6th of November, that is, on that very day on which, seven years before, I had decided once and for all to achieve without fail all the tasks required for my being.

On this day, happening to be in New York, I went early in the morning to the Childs Cafe situated at Columbus Circle, to which I went every morning for my writing.

My American acquaintances, by the way, call this Childs among themselves Café de la Paix, because this cafe here in America has served me during the entire period of my writing activity in the same way as the Parisian Café de la Paix.

That morning I felt like a "mettlesome horse" let loose after having been confined for many months in the stable.

Thoughts were "swarming" in me, chiefly those thoughts pertaining to the work.

Work went so well that by nine o'clock I had succeeded in writing about fifteen pages of my notebook without a single correction.

I probably succeeded so well because, although I should not have allowed any active mentation to proceed in me, I must nevertheless confess that during the last month I had not made much effort, and consequently had considered, involuntarily and half automatically, how to begin this book, which will be not only the last but also the "collected concluding" of all my writings.

At about ten-thirty several of my old acquaintances came in, three of whom are considered there to be writers and sitting down at my table they began to drink their morning coffee.

Among them was one who had worked for me for a good many years on translations of my writings into the English language.

I decided to take advantage of his coming to find out how the beginning of this last book of mine would "sound."

I gave him the pages just written to translate, and continued writing.

We both worked, while the others drank coffee and talked.

At eleven o'clock, in order to rest a little, I asked the translator to read aloud what he had already translated.

When he came, in the translation, to the expression used by me, "intentional suffering," I interrupted his reading, for he had translated the word "intentional" by the word "voluntary."

As I attempted to explain the great difference between the voluntary and intentional suffering of man, there arose a general philological discussion, as is usual in such cases.

In the heat of the argument one of us was called to the telephone.

He came back quickly and announced excitedly that someone wanted to speak to me personally.

I learned from the telephone message that a telegram had just come from London saying that Mr. Orage had died that same morning.

This news was so unexpected that at first, I didn't even take in what it was about.

When I grasped it, however, it fairly struck me.

And it struck me especially because at the same time I remembered certain events connected with this day and with this person.

All at once, there began to be constated in my consciousness various conclusions which I had drawn in my past life, but which had not yet been formed into a conviction, concerning the fact of "noticeable coincidences" which take place in our lives.

In this case, the strangeness of the coincidence showed itself noticeably in that, in this selfsame night, exactly seven years before, as the first of those ideas took form in me on which will be based the contents of the book begun today, I had dictated a letter to just this person and mentioned many of these thoughts.

I had dictated an answer to a private letter from this person concerning the cure for his chronic disease, from which, it seems, he also died.

It was midnight on the 6th of November of the year 1927. I lay sleepless in a whirlpool of oppressive thoughts and, trying to think of something to divert myself a little from my heavy thoughts, I remembered by association, among other things, the letter received a few days before.

On thinking of his letter, and considering his attitude of well-wishing, recently proven to me, I, quite without pity, woke up my secretary who was sleeping in the same apartment and dictated the answer.

At that time Mr. Orage was considered to be, and indeed was, the most important leader in the dissemination of my ideas in the whole northern part of North America.

As in those days I was completely filled with thoughts about my own sickness, and almost entirely convinced of the possibility of regulating my health by means of intentional suffering, I, of course, advised him to do the same but in a form corresponding to his individuality and the conditions of his ordinary life.

I shall not relate here about his further letters and our personal conversations in connection with his illness and my advice; I shall only point out that the essence of the cause of the failure of my advice can be clearly explained to every reader by the words occurring in one of the chapters of this third series, which come from his own mouth.

Among the many unprofitable consequences of this event, namely, the death of Mr. Orage, unprofitable for me and my writings, was also that from that day on, just that 6th of November, for two months, in spite of my constant wish, and constant efforts, I was not able to add a single word to what I had written up to half-past eleven that morning.

And I could not do so thanks to the awakening of one of those factors which arises without fail in the psyche of contemporary people, particularly in Americans, the totality of which causes even the budding of different impulses to become mechanical.

Contrary to the established habits of my former visits, on this stay of mine I had been avoiding all meetings with acquaintances living here, aside from a few people who corresponded to my aim.

But now, each and every one of the great number of people who knew me here, and who learned through the papers or telephone conversations, a usual custom here of the death of my close friend, Mr. Orage, thanks to the said action of the automatically arisen factor, considered it their duty to seek me out in order to express their so-called "sympathy."

And there came and telephoned not only people who were members of that group which Mr. Orage had led, but also people of whose existence I hadn't the faintest idea.

Among these latter were many acquaintances whom, as it turned out, I had met only once and just by chance on my first visit here, eleven years before.

Even in the mornings, when I came to the cafe to work, some Mister or Mistress or other would be sitting there waiting for me.

And no sooner was the He or the She gone than another one would come to my table, and unfailingly with an obviously false, sad face.

Each one of these visitors would "burst" out at once with his "How do you do, Mr. Gurdjieff?" and follow it inevitably with the stereotyped phrase:

"Oh, I am very sorry about Mr. Orage's death!"

What could I answer to this? The question of death is just that question which supersedes all the established and subjectivized conditions of bur life.

In this case, I could not use my usual means for keeping at a distance those visitors who disturbed me at my work.

That would mean the immediate and thoughtless creation of new and eager disseminators of gossip to my discredit.

Even before my arrival in America I had had the intention, as soon as I should begin the writing of this last book of mine, at the same time to make visits, as often as possible, to those states of North America in which groups of people were organized who were followers of my ideas.

In this way, I calculated that simultaneously with the completion at the predetermined time limit of all the tasks I had set myself, I would have completed this last book, as well as the organization of everything required for the dissemination of the first series of my writings.

And therefore, in order to change the circumstances which had arisen which were disturbing my work, I set off as quickly as possible, traveling first to Washington, then to Boston, and from there to Chicago.

But nothing helped, the same thing repeated itself everywhere!

It is perhaps a little understandable that people who knew me in the mentioned cities felt it necessary to express their sympathy to me, as they almost all had known Mr. Orage personally and also his relationship to me.

But the fact that American acquaintances of certain far southern states of North America also began to do this, this was really "stuff and nonsense."

Among the people of the Southern states who expressed their world-famous "sympathy" were those who not only had never seen Mr. Orage but had never even heard of his existence.

They had just learned a few days before that he had died, and that he had been one of my most important assistants.

And thus, among the number of unexpectedly arisen circumstances which prevented me in this period from fulfilling the "Being-task" I had set myself, was suddenly and unexpectedly established this vicious weakness, which has gained citizenship in the general psyche of modern man "to express sympathy."

It has just occurred to me that the thoughts which I expressed to a small group of people at a meeting in a suburb, in connection with the death of Mr. Orage, might serve as a better clarification of the meaning and significance of the whole contents of this chapter, and I have therefore decided to recollect these thoughts in my memory and to add them here.

At this meeting, while drinking coffee, we were speaking of the different habits which take possession of us in our childhood, and which enslave us also after the attainment of mature years.

At this moment there arrived one of their comrades, with a jolly, flushed face. Being late, he had probably been walking quicker than usual, and he had not reckoned on running into me. But as soon as he caught sight of me, the expression of his face changed and, coming up to me, he "burst" out at once with his sentence, learned by heart from the list of "sympathies."

At this point I could no longer contain myself and, turning to them all, said:

"Have you heard the peculiar intonation, not proper to him, with which your comrade who has just come has delivered his bombastic speech?

"Did you? . . . Good. Now then, ask him, that is, beg him, please, for once in his life to make an exception and to say honestly whether his 'inside,' that is, his real being, had any connection whatever with his spoken words.

"Of course, it had none, and how could it be otherwise, for, in the first place, the deceased person concerned in this case was not a 'blood brother' of his and, in the second place, he could not possibly know or feel what attitude the person to whom he addressed his flowery speech had toward the event.

"His words were spoken quite mechanically, without the least participation of his being, and he said them only because, in his childhood, his nurse had taught him in such cases 'to lift the right leg and not the left.'

"But why be insincere even in those cases when there is absolutely no advantage in it for your being, not even for the satisfaction of your egoism?

"Is it not enough that our daily life is filled to overflowing with insincerity, thanks to the abnormally established habits of our mutual relationships?

"Unfailingly to express sympathy at the death of anyone or anybody is just such a vicious habit, instilled in childhood, thanks to the totality of which our half-intentional actions come to an automatic end.

"To express one's sympathy to someone in the case of the death of a person close to him was considered in ancient times an immoral, even criminal action.

"Perhaps it was considered so because it is easily possible that, in the being of that person who is being thus addressed, the process of the fresh impression of the loss of a close person has not yet quieted down, and by these empty words of sympathy he is reminded of it again and his suffering aroused anew.

"From such a habit, customary at the present time in the case of anyone's death, no one derives any benefit, and the person thus addressed, only great harm.

"Such habits, established in contemporary life, offend me especially, perhaps because I have had the opportunity of becoming acquainted with the customs used in the same cases in the lives of people who lived many centuries before us.

"Many thousand years ago, when a person died, for the first three days no one would be present at the place of this sad happening, except the priests and their assistants.

"Only on the fourth day there would assemble all the relations and relations by marriage, as well as neighbors, acquaintances and even strangers who wished to come.

"In the presence of all those assembled, the priests first conducted the religious ceremonies at the door of the house, and then, in the company of all, carried the dead to the graveyard, where they again carried out a special ritual, and then buried him.

"After that, if the deceased was a man, all the men returned to the deceased's house, if a woman, then all the women. All the others separated and returned home.

"Those people who had returned to the house of the deceased first of all ate and drank, but only that food the ingredients of which the deceased himself had prepared during his lifetime for this purpose.

"After this meal, they gathered in the largest room of the house, and set themselves down to the so-called 'Remembering Feast,' recalling to mind and relating only the bad and evil deeds of the deceased during his life.

"And this they did daily for three days.

"After this peculiar three-day procedure, or as one might now call it 'not leaving a good hair on his head,' or as they called it then 'washing the bone of the dead down to the white of the ivory,' all those who had taken part gathered daily in the house of the deceased for seven days, but this time in the evenings after their daily duties were finished.

"During these seven days it was no longer the custom to offer food, but many different sorts of incense were burned constantly in the same room in which the assembly took place, at the cost of the deceased or of his heirs.

"All presents at or kneeled quietly and in the well-known atmosphere called forth by the incense, they first choose from among themselves the worthiest by age and reputation, as leader. And then they began to give themselves up to the contemplation of the inevitability of their own death.

"At certain intervals, the leader would say to all present the following:

'Do not forget how he has lived, whose breath has not yet

vanished from this place, how he behaved unworthily for a man, and did not accept the fact that he, as well as all others, must die.'

"After such an utterance by the leader, all those present had to sing together the following:

'0 ye holy, higher forces, and immortal spirits of our ancestors, help us to keep death always before our eyes, and not to succumb to temptation.'

"I will not add more but will leave it to each one of you to decide for himself what advantage there might be if such a 'savage' custom could be established again.

"I hope that you now partially understand why just these 'expressions of sympathy' of yours affect my inner being almost in the same way as your American 'products' of nourishment affect the English system.

"It would be desirable for all, for God, for the deceased, for you, for me and even for the whole of humanity, if, at the death of any person, instead of the process of the expression of senseless words, the process of the real grasping of your own forthcoming death would take place in you.

"Only the complete realization by man of the inevitability of his own death can destroy those factors, implanted thanks to our abnormal life, of the expression of different aspects of our egoism, this cause of all evil in our common life.

"Only such a realization can bring to birth again in man those formerly present, divine proofs of genuine impulses-faith, love and hope."

As I spoke the above, there occurred to me, I don't know why, the verse of a very old Persian song and, quite involuntarily, I recited it on the spot.

As it had slipped out so involuntarily, I was forced, in order to hide the force of my automatic thought at this moment from the consciousness of those present, willy-nilly, to take the trouble of explaining the contents of these verses of the Persian song in English.

With the words of these ancient Persian verses, a scientific wisdom is expressed, which one may express in your customary language approximately as follows:

If all men bad a soul, long ago there would have
been no room

left on earth

For poisonous plants or wild beasts, and even evil
would have ceased to exist.

Soul is for the lazy fantasy, Luxury for the indulger
in suffering.

It is the determiner of personality, The man and the
link to the Maker and Creator.

Soul is the residue of education, The prime source
of patience.

It is also testimony of the merit of the essence of
eternal Being.

Leader of the will, its presence is "/ am," It

is a part of the All-Being, it was so and,

always will be.

In short, irrespective of my unquenchable wish to work, and irrespective of the fact that at any convenient or inconvenient opportunity I wrote and wrote, so that I might finish this book and attain the end of all the tasks I had set myself, I was, nevertheless, unable to do so.

As (on April 9th, 1935] I had finally finished the prologue, I began on the same day to write this chapter.

And it was in connection with the exposition of this second chapter, on which I am now working, that the coincidence took place, with which I have decided to acquaint the reader, as profitable for this chapter.

The whole day and night of April the 10th, with extraordinary efforts, I worked and reworked the beginning of this chapter, which was unsatisfactory to me, and it was not until the evening of the next day that it seemed as if something was beginning to arrange itself, and the certainty awoke in me that from now on it would be easier.

But, after a few hours of sleep, as I began again to write further, and came to that point where I had first used the expression "problem of the prolongation of human life," I became stuck again.

This time I became stuck because it was suddenly clear to me that for a full explanation of this question which, among all the questions raised by me in this book, I had decided to make the basic question, or as one might say, the "clue," I must without fail, in the first place, if only briefly, inform the reader what position this question takes in present day science and in the mentation of contemporary people.

I began to ponder how to begin, so that the explanation of this question should be as comprehensive as possible, and at the same time not too long.

However, I "turned" the facts, known for this case, and from whatever side I tried to describe them, it all turned out too long.

My thoughts about this introductory theme took such control of me that I ceased to be aware of anything else.

Whoever might come to me, whatever he might say, or with whatever sensations he might leave me, I noticed nothing even my desire for frequent coffee-drinking or cigarette-smoking disappeared.

At times I felt dizzy, as if my head were actually bursting, but I still kept on and on with writing, as if all else depended on it.

On Sunday, the 14th of April, just as it struck midnight, I decided to lie down in the hope of being able to fall asleep, but it was not to be.

It was just the other way. The thoughts, continuing to work, took such proportions that they drove sleep completely away. It became absolutely clear to me that without such an introductory theme everything else would have no worth at all.

Day began to break as I, quite convinced that no sleep would be granted me that day, decided to get up and take a stroll in the streets.

As it was Sunday, and very early in the morning, there was hardly anyone to be seen.

I went down the first street I came to, thinking I might find a night cafe where I could go in and drink a cup of coffee.

As I went, I saw something moving in the distance on the corner and, on approaching, found it was the newspaper dealer laying out his morning "wares."

I decided to buy a newspaper and then go home and lie down again; perhaps by reading the paper my thoughts might be a little distracted, and I might succeed in sleeping, if only a little.

I took *The New York Times*, a huge, thick newspaper, especially on Sundays, but as I paid for it, I realized that reading an English paper would not be the right thing, nor as I do not have the automatic command of this language which comes only with practice give me the desired effect on which I had counted for being able to forget myself and fall asleep.

So, I asked the newspaperman if he, or anyone else in the neighborhood, had European newspapers, for instance Greek, Armenian or Russian.

He answered that he had none, but that three streets further on many Russian Jews were living, and all the newsdealers there had Russian newspapers.

I went in the direction he showed me. Traffic in the streets was beginning to increase.

On the first corner of the designated street was a newspaper booth, to which I went and asked for a Russian newspaper.

The newsdealer asked me at once in Russian, "Which one, countryman, Russkoi Slovo or Russky Golos?"

And thus, I learned for the first time that two newspapers of these names appear in New York.

In order that the reader may discover the necessary connection to this second coincidence here described, I must say in advance that for the last ten years, that is, since I began to write, I have read scarcely anything, not only no newspapers and books but no letters or telegrams either.

I took both Russian newspapers, drove home, and lay down again. One of them was unbelievably thick for a Russian paper, and with

this I began.

On glancing through it, I soon gathered that this paper was celebrating its twenty-fifth anniversary, which explained its thickness.

All the articles in it were so "honeyed" that I put it down and picked up the second.

As I opened it, the first thing on which my eyes fell was this title "The Problem of Old Age," that is, just that question which for the course of three days and nights had left me no peace.

On reading this short article, I was most enthusiastic, and amazed to find in it everything about which I had thought and found necessary as an introduction to what would follow.

And at the same time everything was expressed very compactly, well-formulated and, as the chief thing, unusually objectively.

Involuntarily, I began to consider how I might make use of such a chance coincidence and, after I had thought it over a little, I decided simply to include the entire article in a corresponding place in this chapter.

All the more, as the material given in this article, not being presented by me, would have to be accepted by the readers much more objectively, and therefore with a better result for them.

And in order that quotation of this article may not be considered plagiarism, I am inserting it in full, with information on where it was written and who wrote it, and in addition to that I am underlining the name of the author with two lines.

I was so calmed and cheered up by this article that I determined not to work at all that day, but to go out to see the famous Coney Island, to which I had wanted to go on each previous visit to New York, without ever having succeeded in going there.

THE PROBLEM OF OLD AGE

by
P. MANN

Russky Golos Sunday,
April 14, 1935

When Metchnikov's works were published, it seemed as

if the problem of the prolongation of human life had been solved. According to his view, premature, diseased ageing and death are the results of a chronic poisoning of tissues by the poison of decaying bacteria, which takes place chiefly in the large intestine.

To prolong life, he advised a diet of sour milk (*kefir,* buttermilk), because the bacteria of the milk acid, on their entrance into the intestine, prevent decay as well as the development of the agent of putrefaction.

In proof, Metchnikov gave many examples of longevity of individuals and whole races. The scientist himself lived to be seventy-one years old, an age which none of his family attained, and attributed it to the fact that for several years he had drunk sour milk every day, which was prepared according to a special recipe.

Nevertheless, Metchnikov had exaggerated the importance of the intestinal bacteria. Without doubt, the poisons of the intestinal bacteria are harmful; but there are many still more important causes for the premature ageing of the animal organism. There are certain animals which have no large intestine. But, just the same, they also become old and die.

The causes of premature old age do not lie there. As Metchnikov's theory was rejected by scientists, each brought another theory explaining the causes of longevity in a new way.

The famous French physiologist, Brown-Sequard, attempted to slow down the approach of old age, and to rejuvenate the organism by injections from the sex glands of animals.

After the wide use of this method had shown no great results, Steinach and Voronov, returning to the idea of the French physiologist, tried to achieve rejuvenation by tying back the testicles and grafting on the sex glands of young animals. But they themselves admitted that they attained positive results only in some cases.

And still new theories appear regarding the causes of becoming old: of the physical-chemical changes in the organism, of the wearing out of the blood vessels, and many more.

Each one of them explains in its way the causes of premature ageing and suggests different methods for the prolongation of life. But they are in agreement only in their general conclusion, the conclusion, namely, that death is doubtless in too great a hurry to reach man.

Man can live considerably longer than seventy to seventy-five years, the usual age-length of human life.

How long? And by what means?

It is known that in extraordinary cases man can live to a hundred, a hundred and twenty, and even to a hundred and fifty years! In the Patho-physiological Clinic for the Aged of the Institute of the Union for Experimental Medicine, directed by Professor I. H. Hellman, there is conducted a comprehensive study of the human organism and its different age levels. Apart from minors and adolescents, there are collected here dozens of aged people, of whom some approach the very limits of human age.

More than sixty very old people, men, and women, up to the age of one hundred and twenty-five years, have been in this clinic at one time. Three of them were over a hundred years old. These were: Moschuchin who died a few months ago at the age of 123 years, an aged peasant who could still remember vividly the events of the past century, the feudal estate, the "freed" peasants, he himself receiving ten kopeks a day for his work. The oldest inhabitant of Moscow since Moschuchin's death is Zirulnikov, 112 years, and then Balascheva, 105 years, who was witness to the funeral of Nicholas I.

Among the old people, less than a hundred years of age, is the old "partisan" Aksenova, 75 years old, who took an active part in the Partisan Movement in Siberia and had been driven back more than once through Czechoslovakia, and who had taken part in battles and often made marches of 60 kilometers in 24 hours. Then, there is the foreign language teacher, Pasternatzkaya, 83 years old, who even last year went ice-skating in brilliant competition with the young people.

What have the observations shown? The study of the long-lived has brought us to the conclusion that, aside from the outer, social causes which, for a long span of life, have an enormous part to play, hereditary factors have also a great significance. Almost all the very aged had had completely good health during their whole life! Many of them had retained their memory and their mental faculties. The majority looked much younger than their years. They were never in the least sick.

This characteristic brought the scholars to the extremely important idea of the presence in many of them of inborn immunity to infectious diseases. This biological quality seems to be one of the hereditary factors which characterize those inner conditions under which man may live to a great age.

There are also other extremely important results of the observations. For instance, the observation of the differences between very old and very young people has a great scientific significance. Is the blood of the aged normal?

This question has received a final answer: the blood of the aged has been found to be in a normal state, and to differ very little from the blood of younger people.

At the same time, it has been shown that long-lived people retain their full physical capacity, in particular the sex function, for a very long time.

On comparison of the results of investigations of juveniles and aged, it was possible to establish a fundamental law conformity in the development of man, and to observe functional changes which are determined by the physiological peculiarities of man at different age levels.

The discovery of these laws gives a new possibility for the solution of the problem of old age in general, and of its separate important elements, and especially of that question, which has long interested science, of the preservation to a great age not only of physical but of mental capacity.

Since the work of Brown-Séquard and Metchnikov, this scientific idea has made great progress. The doctrine of the glands of inner secretion has been greatly developed. The latest findings in the field of hormones have brought much that is new. One aim of the work of Professor Hellman's clinic is to make a thorough critical survey of the different scientific theories about the causes of longevity, in order that on this basis they may help to solve the problem of a natural and healthy old age, and to find the way to prolong the life of man.

The work has just commenced. Many investigations, observations, theories, and practical deductions lie ahead. But there is no doubt that the only way to arrive at a solution of this interesting scientific problem is by the comprehensive study of man from birth to old age, the study of the human organism through the combined efforts of physiologists, biochemists, and physicians, as it is being carried out in the Institute of the Union for Experimental Medicine.

This method has opened new and great possibilities to Soviet Russian science.

Now, enough of making use of the extraction from other brains; one must begin again to "suck" from one's own. And thus, every man if he is just an ordinary man, that is, one who has never consciously "worked on himself," has two worlds; and if he has worked on himself, and has become as to say, "candidate for another life," he has even three worlds.

In spite of the fact that everyone, without exception, will certainly think that I have gone completely mad when they read the above statement, I shall nevertheless go on to develop the logical consequences of this ultra-extravagant notion.

If you really want to know the truth, I will tell you how matters stand, and why I pronounced such an absurdity.

First of all, it must be said that in the outpourings of various occultists and other will-less parasites, when they discuss spiritual questions, not everything is entirely wrong.

What they call the "soul" does really exist, but not everybody necessarily has one.

A soul is not born with man and can neither unfold nor take form in him so long as his body is not fully developed.

It is a luxury that can only appear and attain completion in the period of "responsible age," that is to say, in a man's maturity.

The soul, like the physical body, is also matter only, it consists of "finer" matter.

The matter from which the soul is formed and from which it later nourishes and perfects itself is, in general, elaborated during the processes that take place between the two essential forces upon which the entire Universe is founded.

The matter in which the soul is coated can be produced exclusively by the action of these two forces, which are called "good" and "evil" by ancient science, or "affirmation" and "negation," while contemporary science calls them "attraction" and "repulsion."

In the common presence of a man, these two forces have their source in two of the totalities of general psychic functioning, which have already been mentioned.

One of them coincides with that function whose factors proceed from the results of impressions received from outside, and the other appears as a function whose factors issue chiefly from the results of the specific functioning of the organs, as determined by heredity.

In the common presence of a man, as in everything in the Universe, sometimes one and sometimes the other of these totalities of functioning can serve as the source of one of the forces required for the process of which we are speaking.

For this process, it is not important to know which of the two forces is affirmative and which is negative; what matters is that when one affirms, the other denies.

The full realization and precise determination in man of that totality of functioning whose factors are constituted from impressions coming from outside is called the "outer world" of man.

And the full realization of the other totality, whose factors have arisen from automatically flowing "experiences" and from reflexes of the organism notably of those organs whose specific character is transmitted by heredity is called the "inner world" of man.

In relation to these two worlds, man appears in reality to be merely a slave, because his various perceptions and manifestations cannot be other than conformable to the quality and nature of the factors making up these totalities.

He is obliged, in relation to his outer world as well as his inner world, to manifest himself in accordance with the orders received from any given factor of one or the other totality.

He cannot have his own initiative; he is not free to want or not to want but is obliged to carry out passively this or that "result" proceeding from other outer or inner results.

Such a man, that is to say, a man who is related to only two worlds, can never do anything; on the contrary, everything is done through him. In everything, he is but the blind instrument of the caprices of his outer and inner worlds.

The highest esoteric science calls such a man "a man in quotation marks"; in other words, he is named a man and at the same time he is not a man.

He is not a man such as he should be, because his perceptions and his manifestations do not flow according to his own initiative but take place either under the influence of accidental causes or in accordance with functioning that conforms to the laws of the two worlds.

In the case of "a man in quotation marks," the "I" is missing and what takes its place and "fills its role" is the factor of initiative proceeding from that one of the two above-mentioned totalities in which the center of gravity of his general state is located.

The "I" in a real man represents that totality of the functioning of his general psyche whose factors have their origin in the results of contemplation, or simply in the contact between the first two totalities, that is, between the factors of his inner world and of his outer world.

The totality of the manifestations of this third function of the general psyche of man also represents a world in itself, but in this case, it is the third world of man.

And thus, this third world of man is, strictly speaking, as the ancient sciences understood, the real "inner world of man" as opposed to the real "outer world."

I shall call this third definite totality of functioning in the general psyche of man by the same name it was given in the distant past, that is: "the world of man."

According to this terminology, the general psyche of man in its definitive form is considered to be the result of conformity to these three independent worlds.

The first is the outer world in other words, everything existing outside him, both what he can see and feel as well as what is invisible and intangible for him.

The second is the inner world in other words, all the automatic processes of his nature and the mechanical repercussions of these processes.

The third world is his own world, depending neither upon his "outer world" nor upon his "inner world"; that is to say, it is independent of the caprices of the processes that flow in him as well as of the imperfections in these processes that bring them about.

A man who does not possess his own world can never do anything from his own initiative: all his actions "are done" in him.

Only he can have his own initiative for perceptions and manifestations in whose common presence there has been formed, in an independent and intentional manner, the totality of factors necessary for the functioning of this third world.

Thus, it is quite obvious that the whole secret of human existence lies in the difference in the formation of the factors that are necessary for these three relatively independent functions of the general psyche of man.

And this difference consists solely in that the factors of the first two totalities are formed by themselves, in conformity to laws, as a result of chance causes not depending on them, while the factors of the third totality are formed exclusively by an intentional blending of the functions of the first two.

And it is indeed in this sense that one must understand the saying, common to all the old religious teachings, that "man receives all his possibilities from On High."

The necessary factors for the three totalities are formed in man, as is everything in the entire Universe, from corresponding vibrations, whether at a given moment these emanate from the source itself of their arising, or whether they were crystallized previously with a view to further arisings, in accordance with the second fundamental cosmic law, called "the Law of Seven."

To explain what is meant by the vibrations that I have just been speaking about, I can at once take as an excellent example the causes of the fact that today, enemies with an unusual inner attitude toward me are multiplying in great numbers, and I am now in relationship with them on all sides.

Among the diverse characteristic aspects of this unusual inner attitude on the part of the multitude of my enemies, we shall take for our explanation only the following:

There is not, so to speak, a single one of my sworn enemies who, in one or another of his ordinary states, would not be ready to "sell his soul for me."

"What an absurdity!" each of my readers will think. "How could one and the same man possibly have two such diametrically opposed attitudes toward another person?"

Yes, from a superficial point of view, it is absurd and all the same, in reality, it is so.

Indeed, it is an irrefutable fact, a fact that can be demonstrated at will in all its details, not only on the practical level, I mean to say, by normal means available to everybody but also scientifically, by making use of all the "diagnostics" of the various branches of the official science of our day, such as jurisprudence, chemistry, physics, medicine, etc. . . . and, it seems, psychoanalysis itself.

Moreover, nothing is easier to demonstrate than this, in the first place because suitable subjects for study can be found free of charge by the thousands, and furthermore and this is the most important because such investigations have as their point of departure a principle I have already established and formulated in a manner fully acceptable for every category of learned being.

This principle, which is beyond scientific dispute, I have defined in the following terms:

"The sharpness of the contradiction which appears between two diametrically opposed actions is directly proportional to the duration of their meeting."

And, in truth, it is so. The more someone has direct relations with me, the more strength he shows later in the diametrically opposed actions that he manifests towards me.

And this psycho-physical combination, which arises in the reciprocal relations of people, although unbelievable at first sight operates in general in the simple manner which I am about to describe.

First of all, you must know that throughout the entire Universe every concentration, to whatever species it belongs, has the property of giving off radiations.

Given that in man the formation of the three totalities of functioning of his general psyche appears as an arising of results issuing from diverse sources, each of these sources must itself also have the property of giving off radiations.

Just as the radiation of every cosmic concentration consists of vibrations emitted by a corresponding source, so too the vibrations issuing from the processes of each of these quite distinct totalities of functioning that make up the general psyche of man have a density and a degree of vivifying-ness of their own.

When there is a contact between the radiations of different cosmic concentrations, blending of the vibrations takes place according to their "affinity"; similarly, when the vibrations given off by two people come in contact, blending occurs among those of the vibrations that correspond to each other.

In order to explain by analogy certain features of the radiations of a person, I shall take as an example the radiations given off by our Earth.

The general radiations of the Earth, the totality of which manifests as the atmosphere, consist of three independent classes of vibrations, issuing from processes that take place in the very heart of the Earth between metals, metalloids, and minerals.

The general radiation of a person also consists of three independent kinds of vibrations, each with its own quality of vivifying-ness.

And just as the heterogeneous vibrations given off by the Earth encounter certain well-defined limits in the course of their expansion according to their degree of vivifying-ness, so too the different elements of the general radiation of a person have their precise limits.

For example, while the vibrations issuing from a process of active reasoning can, under certain known conditions, acquire a force of expansion that can span hundreds or thousands of kilometers, the vibrations given off by the process of sensation, however active it may be, cannot extend beyond some two hundred meters.

In man, the three kinds of vibrations have their origin in the following three processes:

The first kind of vibrations has its origin in the process called "active thought," and sometimes even, thanks to certain known combinations, in the process of "passive thought."

The second kind of vibrations has its origin in the process called "feeling."

The third kind of vibrations corresponds to the totality of the results issuing from the functioning of all the organs of the physical body, they are also referred to as "vibrations of the instinctive functions."

The vibrations given off by the whole presence of a man in a state of complete relaxation constitute in themselves an atmosphere analogous to the spectrum of colors, having a known limit to its expansion.

And as soon as a man begins to think, to feel or to move, this spectrum like atmosphere changes, both as to the volume of its expansion and as to the quality of its presence.

The greater the intensity of manifestation of one or another of the separate functions of the general psyche of a man, the more the spectrum of his atmosphere is differentiated.

We can very well represent to ourselves the combination of heterogeneous vibrations arising in the general radiation of different persons in the course of their ordinary existence if we compare it to the following picture:

On a dark night, during a violent storm over the ocean, some people on shore observe the oscillations of a floating collection of many-colored electric lamps, connected with each other at long intervals and at the ends with two wires.

Although these colored lamps draw their current from one and the same source, yet since their rays pass through changing conditions of various kinds, some shine out to a distance, others affect each other as they interpenetrate, still others are completely swallowed up either mid-way or at the very place of their arising.

If two people are together, the closer they are to each other, the more intimate is the mixing of their atmospheres, and therefore the better is the contact achieved between their specific vibrations.

The blending and fusion of the specific vibrations given off by different people take place mechanically, depending on their situation in relation to each other and on the conditions, they are in.

And so, among the people with whom I come in contact, the formation of the psychic factors necessary for the manifestation of attitudes diametrically opposed to me must inevitably occur in the following way.

————————

LIST OF TITLES WITH ISBN NO.

ISBN	TITLE
9788194914129	1984
9789390575220	1984 & Animal Farm (2In1)
9789390575572	1984 & Animal Farm (2In1): The International Best-Selling Classics
9789390575848	35 Sonnets
9789390575329	A Clergyman's Daughter
9789390575923	A Study In Scarlet
9789390896097	A Tale Of Two Cities
9789390896837	Abide in Christ
9789390896202	Abraham Lincoln
9789390896912	Absolute Surrender
9789390896608	African American Classic Collection
9789390575305	Aldous Huxley: The Collected Works
9789390896141	An Autobiography of M. K. Gandhi
9789390575886	Animal Farm
9789390575619	Animal Farm & The Great Gatsby (2In1)
9789390575626	Animal Farm & We
9789390896158	Anna Karenina
9789390575534	Antic Hay
9789390896165	Antony & Cleopatra
9789390896172	As I Lay Dying
9789390896226	As You like it
9789390575671	At Your Command
9789390575350	Awakened Imagination
9789390575114	Be What You Wish
9789390896233	Believe In yourself
9789390896998	Best of Charles Darwin: The Origin of Species & Autobiography
9789390896684	Best Of Horror : Dracula And Frankenstein
9789390575503	Best Of Mark Twain (The Adventures of Tom Sawyer AND The Adventures of Huckleberry Finn)
9789390896769	Black History Collection
9789390575756	Brave New World, Animal Farm & 1984 (3in1)

9789390896240	Brother Karamzov
9789390575053	Bulleh Shah Poetry
9789390575725	Burmese Days
9789390896257	Bushido
9789390896066	Can't Hurt Me
9788194914112	Chanakya Neeti: With The Complete Sutras
9789390896042	Crime and Punishment
9789390575527	Crome Yellow
9789390575046	Down and Out in Paris and London
9789390896844	Dracula
9789390575442	Emersons Essays: The Complete First & Second Series (Self-Reliance & Other Essays)
9789390575749	Emma
9789390575817	Essential Tozer Collection - The Pursuit of God & The Purpose of Man
9789390896578	Fascism What It Is and How to Fight It
9789390575688	Feeling is the Secret
9789390575190	Five Lessons
9789390575954	Frankenstein
9789390575237	Franz Kafka: Collected Works
9789390575282	Franz Kafka: Short Stories
9789390575060	George Orwell Collected Works
9789390575077	George Orwell Essays
9789390575213	George Orwell Poems
9788194914150	Greatest Poetry Ever Written Vol 1
9788194914143	Greatest Poetry Ever Written Vol 1
9789390896301	Gulliver's Travel
9789390575961	Gunaho Ka Devta
9789390575893	H. P. Lovecraft Selected Stories Vol 1
9789390575978	H. P. Lovecraft Selected Stories Vol 2
9789390896059	Hamlet
9789390575022	His Last Bow: Some Reminiscences of Sherlock Holmes
9789390896134	History of Western Philosophy
9789390575121	Homage To Catalonia

9789390896219	How to develop self-confidence and Improve public Speaking
9789390896295	How to enjoy your life and your Job
9789390575633	How to own your own mind
9789390896318	How to read Human Nature
9789390896325	How to sell your way through the life
9789390896370	How to use the laws of mind
9789390896387	How to use the power of prayer
9789390896028	How to win friends & Influence People
9788194824176	How To Win Friends and Influence People
9789390896103	Humility The Beauty of Holiness
9789390896653	Imperialism the Highest Stage of Capitalism
9789390575084	In Our Time
9789390575169	In Our Time & Three Stories and Ten poems
9789390575145	James Allen: The Collected Works
9789390896189	Jesus Himself
9789390575480	Jo's Boys
9789390896394	Julius Caesar
9789390575404	Keep the Aspidistra Flying
9789390896400	Kidnapped
9789390896424	King Lear
9789390575824	Lady Susan
9789390896455	Law of Success
9789390896264	Lincoln The Unknown
9789390575565	Little Men
9789390575640	Little Women
9788194914174	Lost Horizon
9789390896462	Macbeth
9789390896929	Man Eaters of Kumaon
9789390896523	Man The Dwelling Place of God
9789390896349	Man The Dwelling Place of God
9789390575909	Mansfield Park
9788194914136	Manto Ki 25 Sarvshreshth Kahaniya
9789390896509	Marxism, Anarchism, Communism
9789390575664	Mathematical Principles of Natural Philosophy

9788194914198	Meditations
9789390575800	Mein Kampf
9789390575794	Memory How To Develop, Train, And Use It
9789390896486	Mind Power
9789390896585	Money
9789390575039	Mortal Coils
9789390575770	My Life and Work
9789390896035	Narrative of the Life of Frederick Douglass
9789390575152	Neville Goddard: The Collected Works
9789390575985	Northanger Abbey
9789390896530	Notes From Underground
9789390896547	Oliver Twist
9789390575459	On War
9789390575541	One, None and a Hundred Thousand
9789390896554	Othelo
9789390575435	Out Of This World
9789390575015	Persuasion
9789390575510	Prayer The Art Of Believing
9789390575091	Pride and Prejudice
9789390896561	Psychic Perception
9789390575381	Rabindranath Tagore - 5 Best Short Stories Vol 2
9789390575367	Rabindranath Tagore - Short Stories (Masters Collections Including The Childs Return)
9789390575374	Rabindranath Tagore 5 Best Short Stories Vol 1 (Including The Childs Return
9789390896622	Romeo & Juliet
9789390896127	Sanatana Dharma
9789390575596	Seedtime & Harvest
9789390896639	Selected Stories of Guy De Maupassant
9789390575206	Self-Reliance & Other Essays
9789390575176	Sense and Sensibility
9789390575299	Shyamchi Aai
9789390896738	Socialism Utopian and Scientific
9789390896646	Success Through a Positive Mental Attitude
9789390575428	The Adventures of Huckleberry Finn

9789390575183	The Adventures of Sherlock Holmes
9789390575343	The Adventures of Tom Sawyer
9789390896691	The Alchemy Of Happiness
9789390575862	The Art Of Public Speaking
9789390896288	The Autobiography Of Charles Darwin
9788194914181	The Best of Franz Kafka: The Metamorphosis & The Trial
9789390575008	The Call Of Cthulhu and Other Weird Tales
9789390575107	The Case-Book of Sherlock Holmes
9789390896110	The Castle Of Otranto
9789390896745	The Communist Manifesto
9789390575589	The Complete Fiction of H. P. Lovecraft
9789390575497	The Complete Works of Florence Scovel Shinn
9789390896820	The Conquest of Breard
9789390896813	The Diary of a Young Girl
9789390896332	The Diary of a Young Girl The Definitive Edition of the Worlds Most Famous Diary
9789390575701	The Great Gatsby, Animal Farm & 1984 (3In1)
9789390575312	The Greatest Works Of George Orwell (5 Books) Including 1984 & Non-Fiction
9789390575992	The Hound of Baskervilles
9789390896707	The Idiot
9789390896714	The Invisible Man
9789390575657	The Knowledge of the holy
9789390575558	The Law & the Promise
9789390896721	The Law Of Attraction
9789390896776	The Leader in you
9789390896363	The Life of Christ
9789390896196	The Man-Eating Leopard of Rudraprayag
9789390896783	The Master Key to Riches
9789390575268	The Memoirs Of Sherlock Holmes
9789390896479	The Midsummer Night's Dream
9789390575466	The Mill On The Floss
9789390896790	The Miracles of your mind
9789390896660	The Mutual Aid A Factor in Evolution
9789390896448	The Origin of Species

9789390896905	The Peter Kropotkin Anthology The Conquest of Bread & Mutual Aid A Factor of Evolution
9789390896806	The Picture of Dorian Gray
9789390896271	The Picture of Dorian Gray
9789390575275	The Power Of Awareness
9789390896356	The Power of Concentration
9788194824169	The Power of Positive Thinking
9789390575411	The Power of the Spoken Word
9788194914105	The Power Of Your Subconscious Mind
9789390896899	The Power of Your Subconscious Mind
9789390896417	The Principles of Communism
9789390575787	The Psychology Of Mans Possible Evolution
9789390896615	The Psychology of Salesmanship
9789390575732	The Pursuit of God
9789390575398	The Pursuit of Happiness
9789390896851	The Quick and Easy Way to effective Speaking
9789390575947	The Return Of Sherlock Holmes
9789390575138	The Road To Wigan Pier
9789390896981	The Root of the Righteous
9789390575855	The Science Of Being Well
9788194914167	The Science Of Getting Rich, The Science Of Being Great & The Science Of Being Well (3In1)
9789390896011	The Screwtape Letters
9789390896073	The Screwtape Letters
9789390575336	The Secret Door to Success
9789390575695	The Secret Of Imagining
9789390896868	The Secret Of Success
9789390896431	The Seven Last Words
9789390575930	The Sign of the Four
9789390896004	The Sonnets
9789390896516	The Souls of Black Folk
9789390896875	The Sound and The Fury
9789390575244	The State and Revolution
9789390896882	The Story of My Life
9789390896936	The Story Of Oriental Philosophy

9789390896752	The Strange Case of Dr. Jekyll and Mr. Hyde
9789390896943	The Tempest
9789390575916	The Valley Of Fear
9789390575879	The Wind in the willows
9789390896080	The Wind in the willows
9789390575763	Their eyes were watching gofd
9789390575831	Three Stories
9789390896950	Twelfth Night
9789390896592	Twelve Years a Slave
9789390896677	Up from Slavery
9789390896974	Value Price and Profit
9789390896967	Wake Up and Live
9789390896493	With Christ in the School of Prayer
9789390575602	Your Faith is Your Fortune
9789390575473	Your Infinite Power To Be Rich
9789390575251	Your Word is Your Wand
9789390575718	Youth
9789391316099	A Christmas Carol
9789391316105	A Doll's House
9789391316501	A Passage to India
9789391316709	A Portrait of the Artist as a Young Man
9789391316112	A Tale of Two Cities
9789391316747	A Tear and a Smile
9789391316167	Agnes Gray
9789391316174	Alice's Adventures in Wonderland
9789391316136	Anandamath
9789391316181	Anne Of Green Gables
9789391316754	Anthem
9789391316198	Around The World in 80 Days
9789391316013	As A Man Thinketh
9789391316242	Autobiography of a Yogi
9789391316266	Beyond Good and Evil
9789391316761	Bleak House
9789391316778	Chitra, a Play in One Act
9789391316310	David Copperfield

9789391316075	Demian
9789391316785	Dubliners
9789391316051	Favourite Tales from the Arabian Nights
9789391316235	Gitanjali
9789391316068	Gravity
9789391316150	Great Speeches of Abraham Lincoln
9789391316662	Guerilla Warfare
9789391316839	Kim
9789391316822	Mother
9789391316211	My Childhood
9789391316846	Nationalism
9789391316327	Oliver Twist
9789391316853	Pygmalion
9789391316334	Relativity: The Special and the General Theory
9789391316389	Scientific Healing Affirmation
9789391316341	Sons and Lovers
9789391316587	Tales from India
9789391316372	Tess of The D'Urbervilles
9789391316396	The Awakening and Selected Stories
9789391316402	The Bhagvad Gita
9789391316303	The Book of Enoch
9789391316228	The Canterville Ghost
9789391316907	The Dynamic Laws of Prosperity
9789391316006	The Great Gatsby
9789391316860	The Hungry Stones and Other Stories
9789391316433	The Idiot
9789391316440	The Importance of Being Earnest
9789391316297	The Light of Asia
9789391316914	The Madman His Parables and Poems
9789391316457	The Odyssey
9789391316921	The Picture of Dorian Gray
9789391316464	The Prince
9789391316938	The Prophet
9789391316945	The Republic
9789391316518	The Scarlet Letter

9789391316143	The Seven Laws of Teaching
9789391316525	The Story of My Experiments with Truth
9789391316532	The Tales of the Mother Goose
9789391316549	The Thirty Nine Steps
9789391316594	The Time Machine
9789391316600	The Turn of the Screw
9789391316983	The Upanishads
9789391316617	The Yellow Wallpaper
9789391316426	The Yoga Sutras of Patanjali
9789391316990	Ulysses
9789391316624	Utopia
9789391316679	Vanity Fair
9789391316020	What Is To Be Done
9789391316686	Within A Budding Grove
9789391316693	Women in Love

www.ingramcontent.com/pod-product-compliance
Lightning Source LLC
Chambersburg PA
CBHW020911070526
44654CB00002B/23